GABRIELLE

GABRIELLE

by Robert Ansell

RAVEN RECORDING, INC.

WWW.RAVENRECORDING.COM

Published by Raven Recording Inc.
New York City
www.RavenRecording.com

All photos by Robert Ansell, unless otherwise credited.
Designed and edited by Nilaya Sabnis

ISBN 978-1-0880-6291-3

This book is dedicated to Gabrielle, my sons – Scott, Brian, Kevin and Jonathan, and my grandchildren – Sofia, Luke and Ava. Without them, what would it all matter?

And, special thanks to Gil and Joanne for introducing me to Gabrielle and to Gil for the kick in the butt to write.

And, my deepest thanks and love to Nilaya for everything she is to me and everything she does for me.

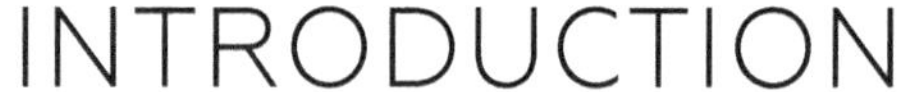

INTRODUCTION

Welcome to my therapy. I am probably doing this for my own benefit. I don't think it's about closure – I'm not ready for that yet. Although it's been two years since Gabrielle passed, I don't really feel alone. Because of her teaching schedule, I became quite used to being without her in my physical presence. She could be gone for 3, 4 or sometimes 5 weeks. When people asked her about our relationship, how we could be apart for such long periods of time, she always answered: "We're never apart." And, in fact, we have not been apart these past two years – she is so deeply ingrained in my heart, mind and bone marrow.

As far as I am concerned, she's still here. I'm constantly amazed at the depth and strength of her presence in my life and that of others. I feel that I'm still sharing my life with her. But, I am beginning to get the point the she is not coming back next week from teaching a workshop in Switzerland, although I still wear my wedding ring and don't put my feet up on the coffee table – just in case.

These memories come to me daily and randomly; I have tried to organize them, to give them a context. This is not an attempt, by any means, to be a definitive biography or to memorialize the inspirational and catalytic effect she had on tens of thousands of others, or to present an exhaustive list of her accomplishments or personality. That is a task requiring far more intelligence than I can muster at any given moment in time. Gabrielle wrote 3 books exploring her philosophy, perspective and 5Rhythms® practice, and they are the grail for anyone interested in that journey. She viewed life through the prism of rhythm and used movement to change consciousness, unravel the psyche and explore the human condition.

I should end this beginning with an apology. I think this is going to be expensive for such a thin book, but I want to print a lot of photographs and reproduce them well. It's all to a good cause – **Long Live the 5RRO!**[1]

---

[1] 5Rhythms Reach Out is a not-for-profit company Gabrielle formed to bring the healing power of rhythm to those in need. It will benefit from the sales of this book.

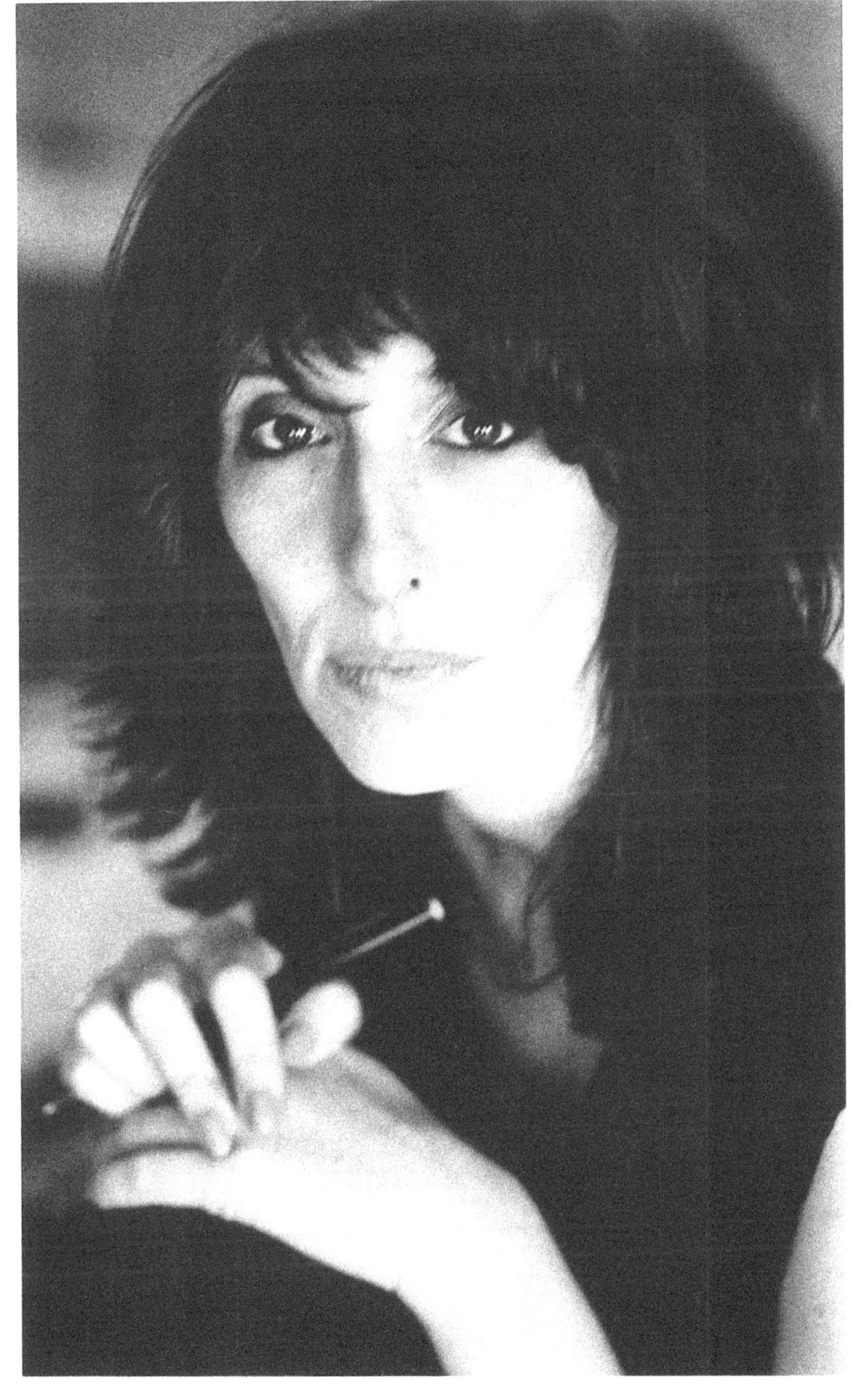

GABRIELLE ROTH WAS...

MY LOVE

In order for me to meet Gabrielle, a young man had to walk into an intensive care unit in a New Jersey hospital and kill his older brother with a shotgun blast to the head.

The older brother had been paralyzed from the neck down in a motorcycle accident and begged his brother to end his misery. As he said, he could not face life as a "head in a bed". I was a criminal defense lawyer at the time and was hired to defend the young man. The case drew intense and national attention and, shortly after I was retained, I got a call from a novelist (Judy) in Los Angeles who wanted to venture into her first attempt at non-fiction with a book about this case. I negotiated the deal and we used the money from the book advance to fund the defense.

Judy spent the pre-trial months with me and my family and we became dear friends. A year or two after the trial, she called to say she thought it important that I register for a two-week meditation program in the California desert. It sounded a little weird and "New-Agey" to me. I didn't really know or care much about meditation, but some vacation time in the desert seemed interesting. It was weird. On my first night there, one of the participants told me he had just come from Las Vegas. When I asked if he had gambled, he responded that he was simply "processing his money space." Whew!

One of the best things about the experience was meeting and befriending Gil, a financial manager for many show business luminaries in LA. We became close and stayed in touch. I later learned that he and his wife, Joanne, were very dear friends with Gabrielle.

About one year later (April, 1977 to be exact), Gabrielle, who was living in Marin County at the time, called Joanne in LA to ask if they wanted to go to Palm Springs for a few days. Joanne didn't think it was possible, but called back in a few hours to say: "You won't believe this, but one of Gil's clients is buying a house in Palm Springs and asked if we would go down and stay there a few days to check it out." Gabrielle was delighted to join them.

It was an important weekend for Gil and Joanne. They had bought a beach lot in Malibu and were going to begin construction of a magnificent house the following Monday. After returning from Palm Springs, they planned to have a ceremony at the beach lot on Sunday to ritualize the event.

On Thursday night in Palm Springs, Gabrielle announced to Joanne and Gil that she was through with men. She had recently had a bad experience and thought it best to concentrate on her spiritual life as a teacher. Joanne vigorously protested and told Gabrielle that she had to focus. "Make a list of the qualities you want in a man," she said, "and we'll put that out into the universe. "On a piece of scrap paper, Gabrielle wrote that he had to be tall, have his own children (she had a six-year old son, Jonathan), be Jewish (not sure where that came from – she wasn't) and be a lawyer. Something like Gil. They returned to LA on Saturday.

On Sunday, I flew into LA as I had been doing monthly for several years. I had a client in business there and the routine was to fly out one day, work one day and fly back to NJ the next to attend to my trial practice. For some reason on that Sunday, I called Gil to see if he wanted to go out for a drink. This was totally out of character for me. I never "go out for a drink". I certainly have a cocktail or wine with a meal, but the practice of going somewhere to just drink was foreign to me. I had been going to LA for years and never thought to call Gil. But, on this particular Sunday, I made this particular call, to this particular person, for this particular reason.

Gil said he couldn't go out with me, but would love for me to come to their lot in Malibu at 3:30 to participate in their ground-breaking ceremony. He had a very old and very expensive bottle of French wine to commemorate the event. To make it even better, Judy and her husband would be there, along with a friend from Marin County who was staying at their house. I learned later that when Joanne went to the guest room to get Gabrielle for the ride to Malibu, she said that a friend of theirs from NJ would be attending and: "He's a lawyer!"

April 17, 1977. 3:30PM. I arrive at the lot to greet my four old friends and meet Gabrielle. I was immediately fascinated. I had never met anybody whose body was so connected to her words. Listening was secondary – I actually found myself watching her talk. And those eyes! They changed color on a dime and intensity in a flash.

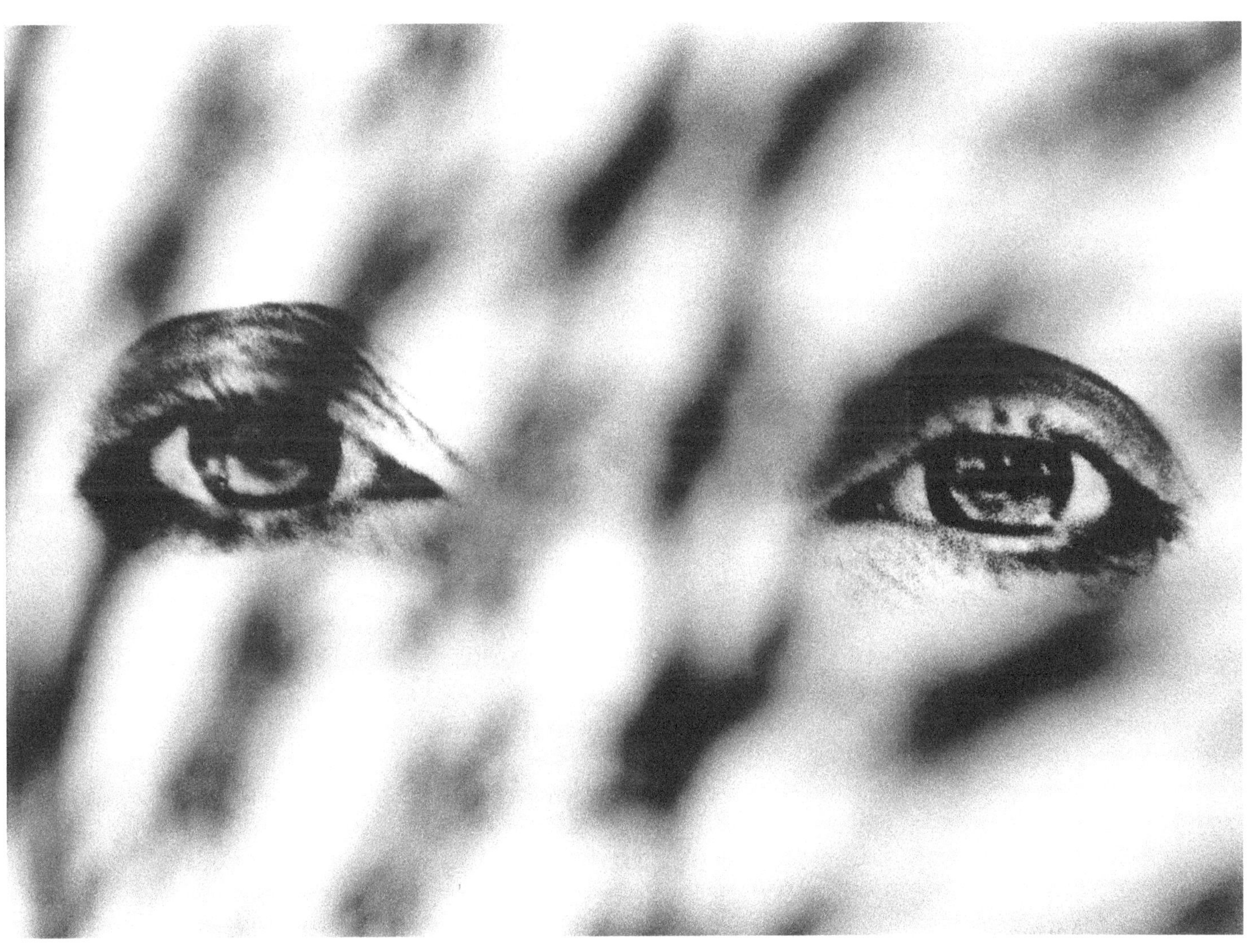

It was a little cool at the beach and she was kind to share her serape with me. She smelled great. The wine didn't; it had turned to vinegar.

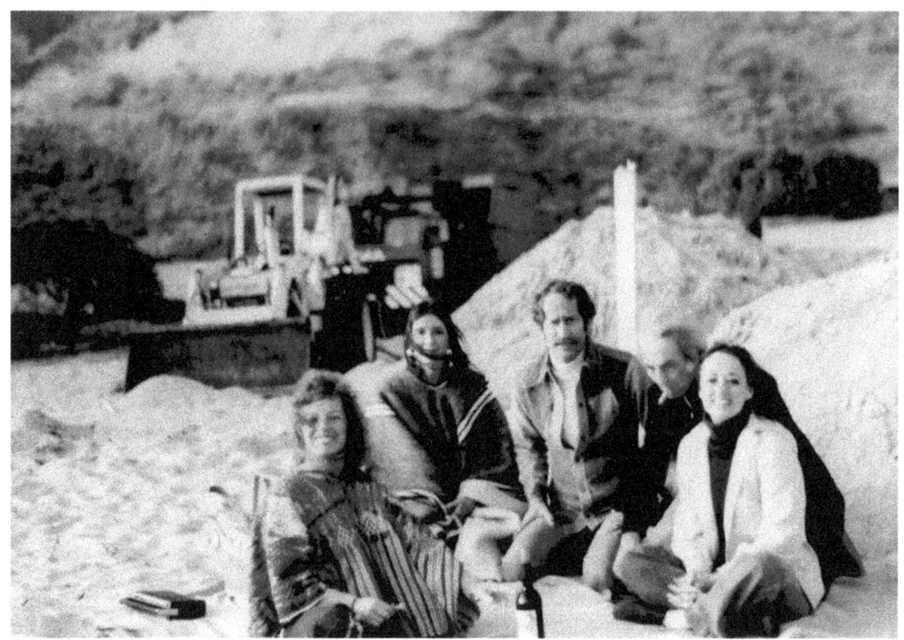

photo by Gil Segel

This photo was taken about one hour after we met. I was doing my Starsky & Hutch impersonation at the time. It was cold that day in Malibu and our first physical contact was when she shared her serape with me. And, this was the first time I saw her with her hair in her face. I came to learn, of course, that with the way she moved, she always had her hair in her face.

After some time at the beach, I joined them for coffee at a nearby café. I couldn't stay long because I had a date that night in Marina del Rey. My fascination with this Gabrielle person was tangible, but I could not manage to make any significant contact even though

I was seated directly across the table from her. She and Judy's husband were in an intense conversation and it would have been rude to interfere. But, I heard her mention that she was getting an astrology reading the next morning and, all of a sudden, I developed this intense interest in astrology. Truth be told, I didn't know astrology from astronomy, but I asked her to call me after her reading. If she felt good about it, I would be interested in one. Talk about manipulation!

She called around noon on Monday to say she was unhappy about the reading. The astrologer told her she was several planets removed from Earth, should be winning Oscars as an actress and would never find a soul mate because she had too much high priestess energy. As she put it: "I just spent $250 to be told that I'm weird, in the wrong occupation and will be alone for the rest of my life." I asked her to lunch.

And, we have been together from that moment on, from that lunch to the day she passed on October 22, 2012. Absolutely together. No doubts. No questions. No processing. No therapy. No separations, trial or otherwise. Together! 35 ½ years. Sure, we could bicker with the best of them, but never for long and never with malice. And never where our relationship was at stake. Our relationship was never at stake. We were a couple.

We are mirrors of the best and worst in each other...Sometimes we get stuck in the same patterns—the angular, brittle movements, the icy silence all turned in on itself, the pretense it's not happening, the dark sighs and feigned willingness to hear each other out.

In other words, sometimes we're pathetic. Just last week his "victim" pattern was competing with mine for supremacy. We caught ourselves and laughed. That's the beauty of time and repetition.[2]

And, when someone would later ask her how she knew I was "the one", she would point to a moment in the kitchen of Judy's house where we went after that first lunch.

Robert was leaning against Judy's sink and I was standing about two feet in front of him, telling her how we met, when I felt his energy in the small of my back. It was so strong I got caught between two words in my own sentence. In this short, sweet space, I felt his dream merge with mine and roll right off my tongue. Suddenly this very ordinary event seemed quite cosmic.

This man was different. I couldn't see the end. I could always see the end hanging around the shadows on the other side of the first kiss. Not this time. This time I knew I could really be hurt. I talked myself down from terror by reminding myself that if he left me I would write some broken-hearted poetry, do some dangerous dancing, and learn a powerful lesson. And, if he stayed, I'd do the same thing with a different twist. So, what was the fuss about?

By the way, I am tall, Jewish, have my own children (three incredible sons) and was, when I met her, a lawyer.

[2]This and later italicized sections are excerpts from Gabrielle's contribution to a book on couples in long-term relationships called *We Two*, edited by Roger Housden and Chloe Goodchild and published in the UK by The Aquarian Press in 1992.

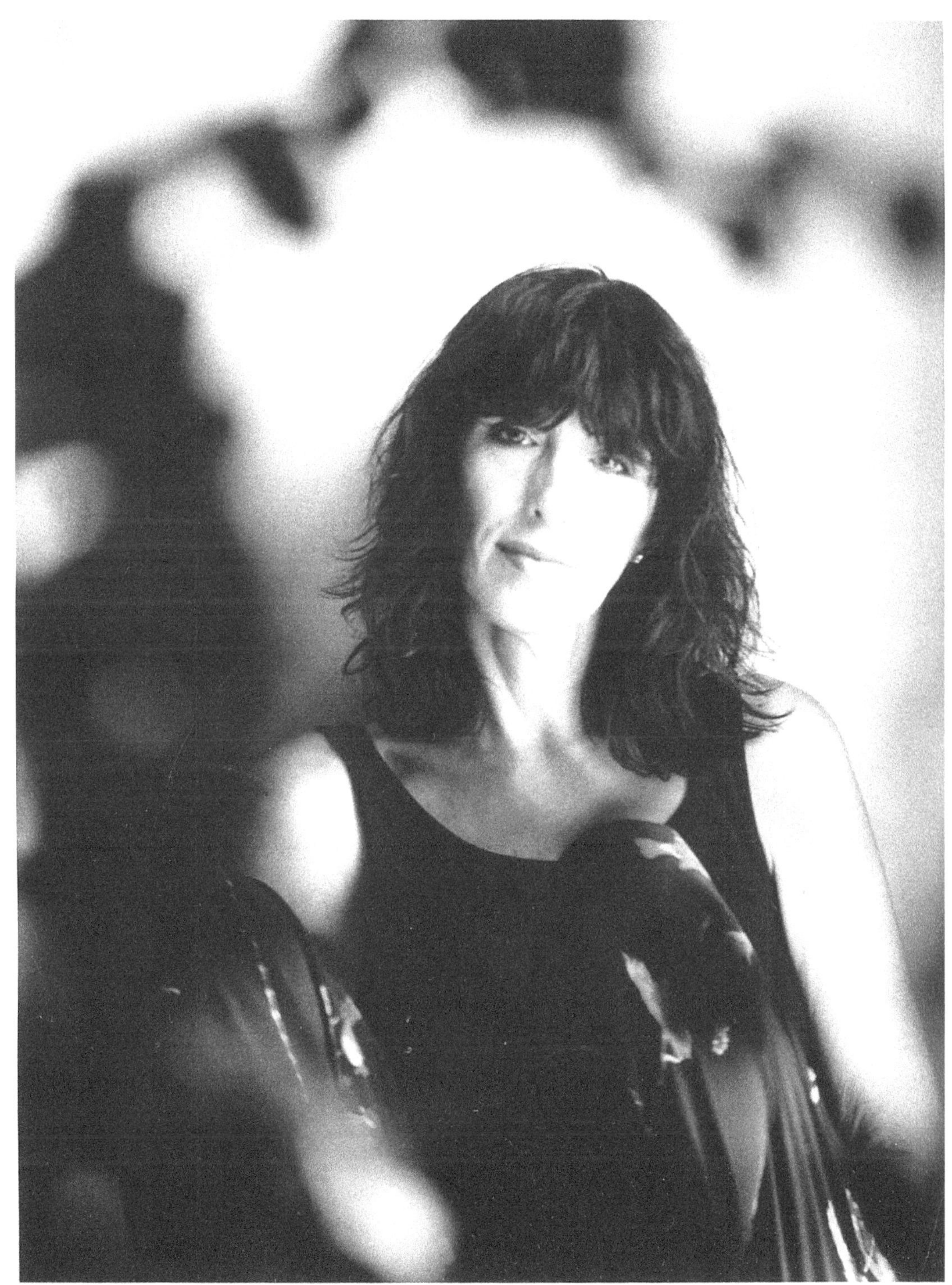

MY WIFE

Actually and officially getting married was never important to either of us. We were MARRIED and no piece of paper was going to make a difference. We never even talked about it; it just didn't matter.

But, about 6 years into our relationship, the world started to creep up on us. Mainly, the US government (our income tax situation was terrible because we could not file a joint return) and the medical industry (my health insurance did not cover my non-wife). So I surprised Gabrielle with a proposal in Room 4 of Esalen Institute on the Friday evening before a weekend workshop she was teaching. And, lo and behold, she said "Yes." Actually, despite our former indifference, we both got excited and began to plan the wedding. It was going to be small – just the children and a few very close friends.

This was not as easy as we had first thought. Gabrielle was the queen of ritual, after all, and the outside expectations were intense. And who would officiate at the ceremony was a decision that had all kinds of ramifications. I was seriously anti-religious and did not want to have clergy of any kind involved. She didn't care about that, but was concerned about choosing among various friends who qualified for the position and disappointing those not selected. Let's find a Zen-Buddhist priest, she suggested and I agreed.

Unfortunately, the date of our proposed wedding was also the weekend that the Dalai Lama was conducting a conference in upstate New York and all local Zen-Buddhist priests were going to be out of town. But Gabrielle contacted a small center in NYC and found that a brand new Zen priest, just arrived from Korea, was going to be in town. We met with him on the Tuesday before the Saturday wedding. He didn't speak a word of English, had no relationship skills, and seemed to be as interested in this event as I was in the state of Shintoism in the Canary Islands. But, we got through the conference and learned from his interpreter that we would need seven white flowers, 3 pieces of fruit that were not peaches (something about the fuzz I do not understand to this day), and would be obliged to invite all members of that Zen temple who wanted to attend.

We booked plane tickets and hotel reservations for London and Paris and invited the children. When Gabrielle told my mother about our plans (something I had told her was not a good idea), my mother kind of freaked out. "A Zen-Buddhist priest?" she asked. "What am I going to tell my friends?" I told Gabrielle to suggest that she tell her friends we were married by the Chief Rabbi of Israel. Gabrielle declined that suggestion and the exchange put a damper on the proceedings.

We decided to cancel the wedding. But, on that Saturday, we had dinner with the children and my parents at a wonderful romantic restaurant in the city and left the next day for our "honeymoon" in Europe. And, a few years later (eleven years after we first got together), we went to City Hall with two of the kids and did the official deed. Not very romantic. After the City Clerk did his job, I went to work.

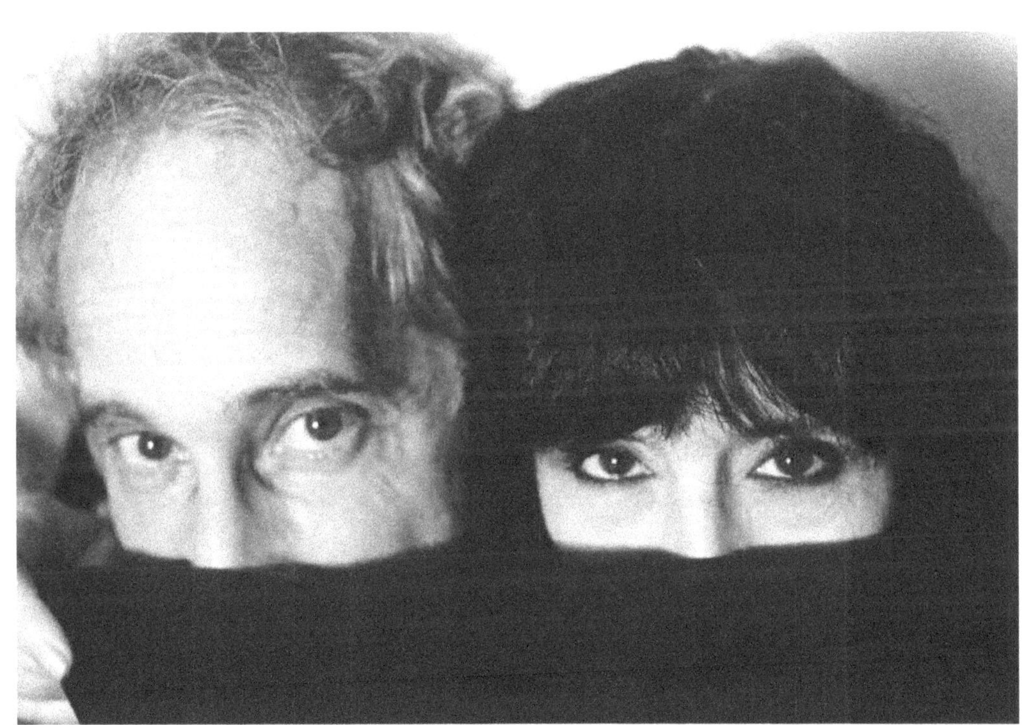

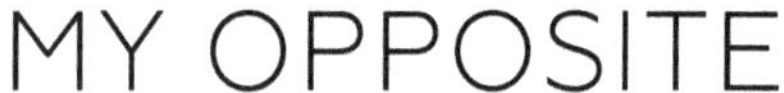
MY OPPOSITE

It is somewhat amazing that Gabrielle and I were together so long and well. Our psyches were reverse images (although she used to say that we were each other inside out).

CREATIVE PROCESS

When Gabrielle was faced with a creative problem or possibility, she immediately made it a communal project, putting it "out on the table", asking others for their opinions and contributions, bouncing possible solutions off of each other. I, on the other hand, was freaked out by that process. Give me something creative to do and I go off into the corner, by myself, sharing nothing with anybody until I had taken it as far as I could go without anyone's help or contribution.

EGOS

My ego lives in the past while Robert's roams the future. He projects himself into space and figures out all the variables, while I rehash and rearrange what's already gone down.

It's true. I back into parking spaces, ready to leave when I arrive.

IDEAS

An idea to Gabrielle was a chance to soar, to take it and fly as high and far as possible, to immediately set in motion the pursuit of all of its possibilities and extremities, remote or otherwise. Give me an idea and all I want to do is grab its four corners and reduce it immediately into a neat knot.

She wanted to set a thought loose. I wanted to capture it.

MONEY

When we were short, I wanted to spend less. Gabrielle's focus was to make more. And, as she put it:

I spend; he saves.

SURPRISE

As a litigator, a criminal defense lawyer, surprise was my deadly enemy. The idea, always, was to know what was going to happen in the courtroom or make happen what you decided in advance should happen. I believed that a lawyer who was surprised in the courtroom was guilty of malpractice.

Gabrielle loved surprise, in her life and, most incredibly, in her work. She never planned the details or outcome of a workshop or class. Of course, she was somewhat limited by the title of the event, something she had to provide months in advance for PR and registration purposes. But, titles were malleable to her; it was the moment that always ruled. Of course, if the workshop was entitled, HEARTBEAT, she was committed to it dealing with emotions. But, that was it. She would enter the room with no idea what exactly she would say to the people, what exercises she would use, what music would be played. She used to tell me that she didn't know in advance what would actually happen in a workshop because she didn't know who would be there, what they were feeling, etc. She went into a workshop to see what would happen, not to make something specific happen.

She said it best one night in Vermont. She was scheduled to address a large group of corporate financiers, lawyers, accountants, comptrollers, etc., the next morning and, not only that, but get them to dance! As we got into bed, I asked what she was going to say to these folks in the morning. "No idea," she said. I told her she was crazy, that I couldn't imagine going into that situation without a script. "Well, Rob," she said as she turned out the light. "After you jump and before you land, is god."(I turned on the light and wrote it down.)

The next morning, they danced.

They always danced. She thought of her work as a seduction; not to attract people to her, but into themselves, their curiosity, their wildness, their freedom. At bottom, what could she do to lure people into their bodies? I remember a rehearsal we had for a one-song gig in New York City back in 1980. We had to hire a few new musicians for this and, at the run-through, Gabrielle announced to the band that this is the part of the song where the people would dance. The new bass player leaned over to me and said: "Doesn't she know this is New York? People aren't going to dance."

They danced. And, when they did, the bassist got my attention and mouthed the word "sorry!"

She loved to take chances. As she said: "If you're not living on the edge, you're taking up too much space."

RHYTHMS

Gabrielle's "home" rhythm was Flowing (with her moon in Stillness). Mine is Staccato. She used to refer to me when trying to explain Staccato to her students: "Just look at his desk. All the pens and pencils and pads are all lined up!" When we went to the movies, I would be standing in the elevator pushing the button, while she was still in the apartment putting on her shoes. Initially, of course, I would make her "wrong" for this, but after doing the 5Rhythms work, I came to see it as just a difference, not a deficiency. I learned a lot about Flowing from her and she learned a lot about Staccato from me.

ADDICTION

Gabrielle could let go. During our time together, she let go of tobacco, coffee, recreational drugs, sugar, alcohol, meat, vegetarianism. Some of this was health-related, some about life style, some as an experiment to check her energy response. But not tea! No way. Tea was a constant. It was amazing how much comfort she could find in a cup of tea.

I, on the other hand, am addicted to sugar, caffeine and carbs, and pray to the Goddess Nicotina. Being a bit of a control freak, I spend much focus on dealing with them. Gabrielle told me that I was addicted to controlling my addictions.

MORE

She was very open emotionally; I am not. She was creative; I am analytical. She shopped; I don't.

I ponder decisions, Robert makes them on the beat and doesn't look back. I save things, he shreds them. When he finishes a meal, he's ready to run. I enjoy lingering over tea and conversation. He wants to taxi home; I prefer walking. He arrives at airports an hour early; I get there just on time... He grew up in the same place and I grew up in several. I moved, he stayed still and we met anyway.

The beauty of it all was that we never competed, except, of course, for what movie to go see. (We were opposite there too. I go for chick-flick, rom-coms; she went for dark, heavy literate stuff.) We didn't try to impose our patterns and perspectives on each other, but saw our differences as a strength, something we could give to each other and learn from each other. Despite or because of all those contradictions, we found a way to move through the world gracefully (her) and clumsily (me) together, as a team, finding harmony in the polarities.

We were the same in one way – lone wolves. She was. I am. She was always surprised that she made her living in groups. It's amazing that we allowed each other to live with each other. Although, on reflection, the reason we stayed together may very well be that when I related to her, I took on some of the more essential qualities of a cocker spaniel.

MY BETRAYER

Naaahhh! I don't think so. I can't even imagine it. But, if she ever did cheat on me, the guy had a Harley parked outside and he looked like the long lost son of James Dean and George Clooney.

Me betray her? Not on your life – or mine. I knew I was married to a shaman and this is no energy to mess with. All she had to do was cast one spell and I could awaken some morning with my left testicle a distant memory.

Except, of course, for Bertha.

Bertha, my drum and mistress, is at the bottom of 16 albums and kept me company while Gabrielle was away teaching. Gabrielle was very open-minded and accommodating about my love affair with her.

Here are my wife and girlfriend in the same photos.

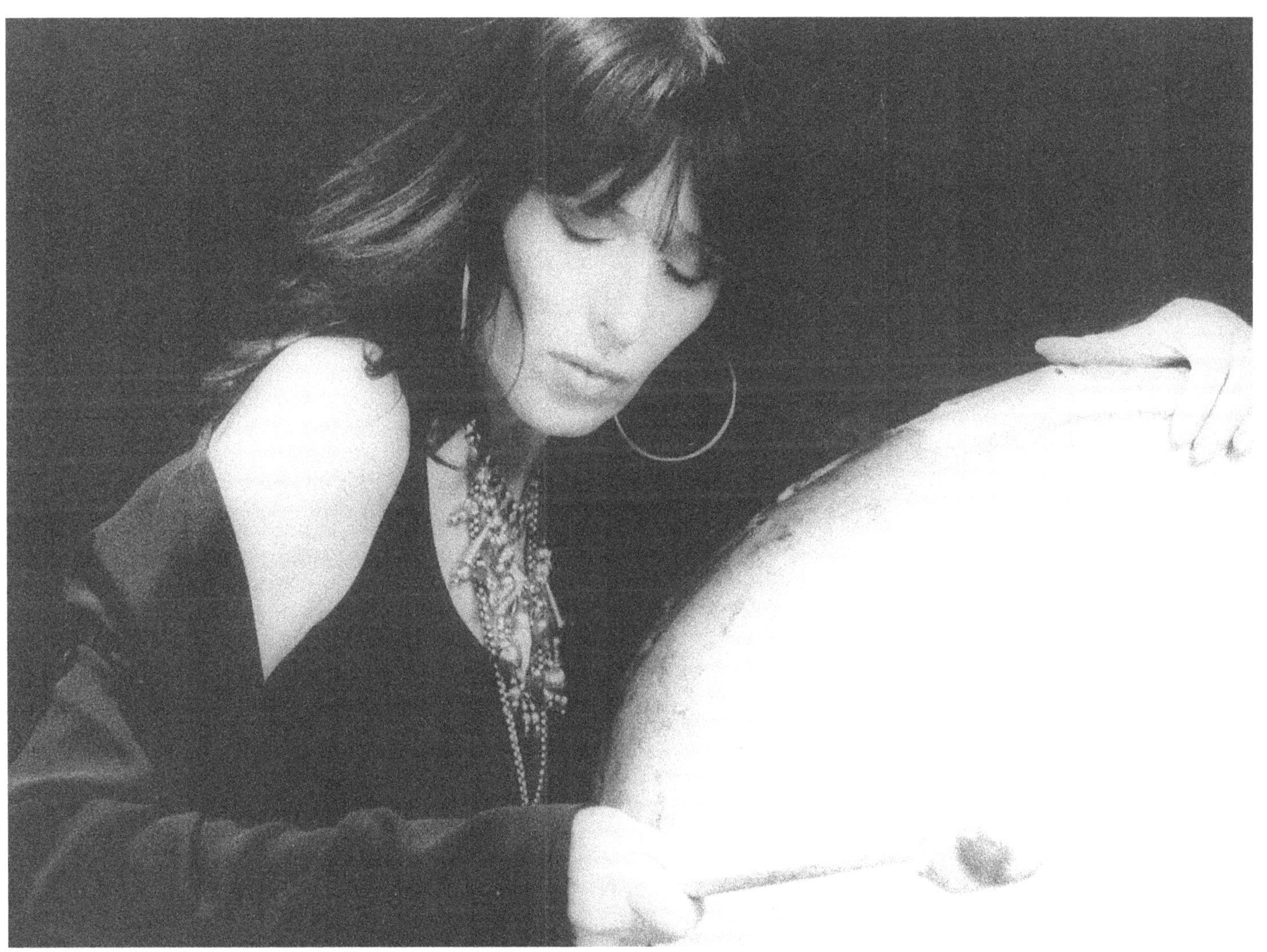

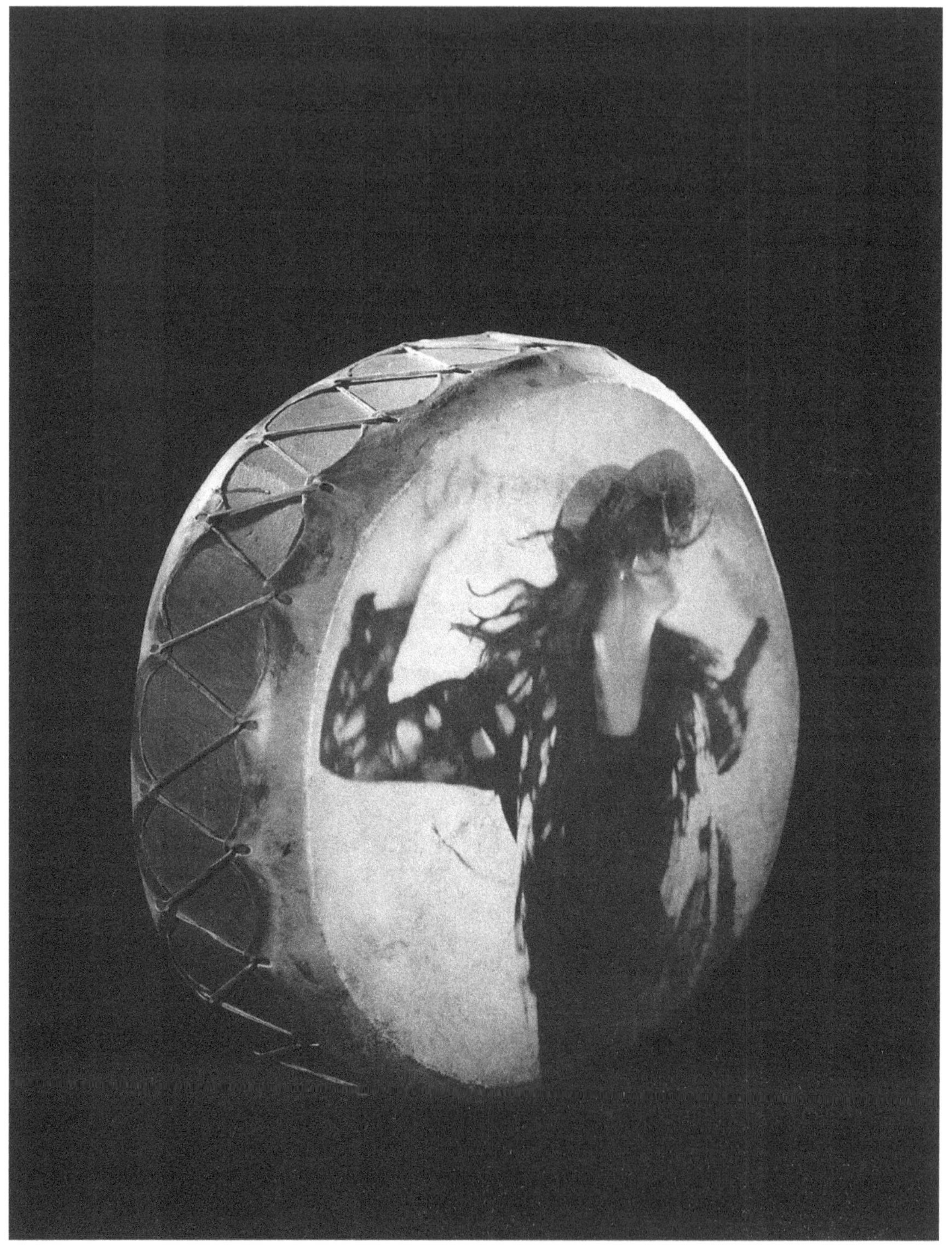

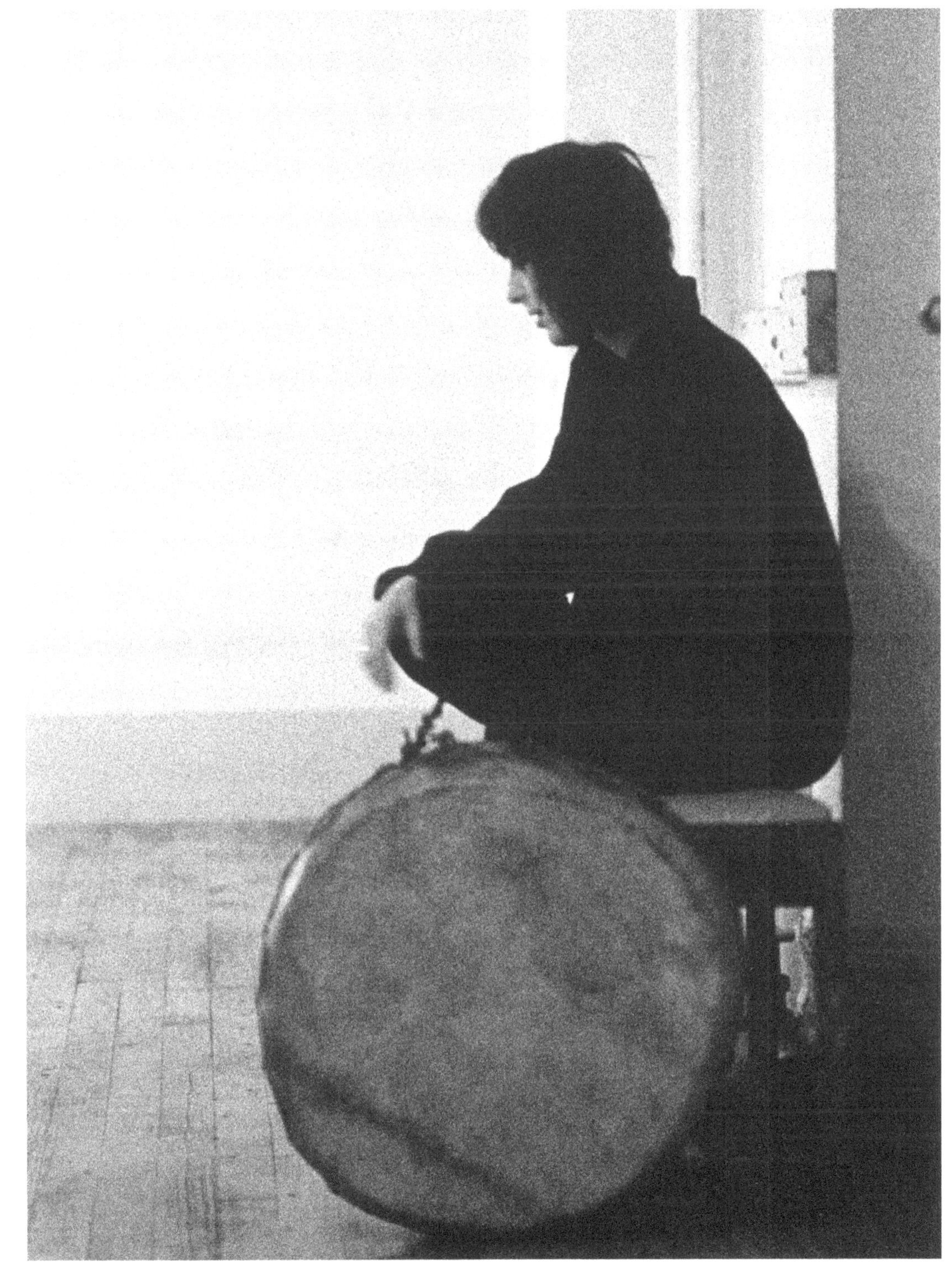

A MOTHER

Robert had three sons, I had one, and we had four. We were a part-time family, three of us during the week, except on Wednesdays, and six on the weekends. …

Kids don't become friends, much less brothers, because two people fall in love. Especially when one of those kids is getting what the others want most desperately, their own father's attention and time... Sorting out the feelings of kids from a fragmented family was my hardest task.

Every weekend we had a houseful of kids and our time together included them. No babysitters, no dates, no introductions and awkward endings. Instead, I had someone to cook with, someone to stand in movie lines with, someone to follow around at museums and zoos, someone to roll my eyes at during parent/teacher meetings, someone to cuddle with while we watched tv.

It was actually through Gabrielle that I stopped thinking of my children as a group. This was a profound change in me as a father. Somehow, I had gotten it into my head that they should do and be everything together, whether it was going to camp, playing a sport, keeping visitation – everything – one size fits all.

Scott – sound engineer who was instrumental in our recording and in the foundation of Raven Recording. Solid, responsible, sweet – the part of me that is kind, gentle and found the heart to be in total service to Gabrielle through the final journey. She was instrumental in our helping Scott achieve his "unorthodox" dream of becoming a sound engineer in a family of lawyers and doctors.

Brian – lawyer. He is taking my footsteps to the next level. Bold and forceful, the part of me that moved confidently through the world and built a fascinating legal career. She was instrumental in understanding his position and fostering his independence.

Kevin – a guitarist, a little more soul than rock 'n' roll, and the part of me that gave it all up to be a percussionist. She was instrumental in encouraging him to follow his musical dream and destiny.

Jonathan – I got this one the easy way – no ob/gyn fees, smelly diapers, pre-school, etc. It didn't take long for him to become my son and dear friend:

My kid recognized him in the first three seconds. Most often, when I introduced my six-year old son to the man of the moment, he'd stand up straight and shake his hand. He took one look at Robert and began jumping up and down on the bed in total bliss.

Was he acting out my true response, the one underneath the I'd-better-be-cool-cause-I'm-losing it act?

My kid was the period on the sentence. I looked up into the sloe-blue eyes of Mister Right.

I guess I owe Jonny. I owe all of my children – they are the foundation and background of my movie, the constant theme of my inner life.

"Mother" meant more to Gabrielle than just taking care of children. A lot of her work focused on the maternal instinct, the automatic response to the question: "What do I need?" She learned how to mother herself and then helped others do the same.

And, she had a compelling maternal instinct when it came to the Certified Teachers of 5Rhythms work. Her constant focus was on their well-being and woe be to anyone who tried to take any liberties with them or her work. She was the "protector" and, with my legal background, I became the "enforcer", not the most popular kid on the block. Better me than her, though, and I know she appreciated the buffer zone my presence created for her.

Twenty-five years ago, she told me I needed to work on my maternal instinct – it should be a cat, something to be responsible for, to feed, groom, supervise and clean up after. So, of course, three days after she mentioned it, we got a call from a flute player we hadn't heard from in years to ask us whether we wanted a kitten that had been abandoned in the lobby of her building.

And, about three months before she was diagnosed, she pulled another one of her "G-strings" (she seemed to have a way of tugging at the threads of the universe to accomplish amazing things) by encouraging me to learn to cook. Prior to this, the only time I went into the kitchen was to order something. She was a good cook but gave it up after Jonny left the nest. We ate out almost every night. Early on, we started the practice of taking out the food we didn't eat. Between the restaurant and our walk home (sometimes, as many as 40-50 blocks), we knew we would run into someone who needed that food for dinner more than we needed leftovers. It got to the point that we would leave the house, go left to the corner of 13th and University, and the homeless guy would say: "Great. Where are you folks eating tonight?"

The timing of my becoming a cook was horribly perfect. As my ability to cook grew, her ability to go out deteriorated. It was as if she knew what was coming. So, I cooked, shopped and juiced for her and, basically, became responsible for her well-being. She would laugh and tease me: "You're not only my husband; you've become my Mother."

A PSYCHIC

I was never very enamored of what Gabrielle called the "Crystal Ball crowd". I have no doubt that we know things that we do not know that we know. But, accessing that knowledge is quite another matter. I believe, for example, that we are influenced in subtle ways by the mass and gravitational pull of the stars and planets. I do not believe that means they can tell me to wear a blue shirt next Tuesday if I want to be successful in life.

MOTHER EARTH

Gabrielle has written about several of her psychic episodes involving weather, so no need for me to repeat them. But the first one I experienced has not been told.

When she first moved to New Jersey, I lived in a town house in Sea Bright, a narrow peninsula of land between the Atlantic Ocean and the Navesink River. I loved being so close to the ocean – there was my house, a narrow street, a sea wall and the ocean, with a narrow strip of beach depending on the tide.

It was 7:30 on a December morning, a couple of months after she moved east. There was a very light snow falling and a moderate amount of wind – nothing unusual for December. This was long before weather channels and Dopler graphics. I was leaving the house to go to court when she asked me not to go. She felt in danger. I was in the middle of a trial and could not simply stay home without calling the judge to offer a reasonable excuse. But she was scared. I forget now what story I made up (I couldn't tell the judge that my wife had a strange premonition), and got excused for the day. Nothing much happened until about 3:30 PM when I looked out the window and saw water coming over the sea wall. It was green water. I had seen white water (foam) come over occasionally, but never green. I called the police department to find out when high tide would be over and they told me that high tide would not be coming for 2 more hours.

We ended up being evacuated later that afternoon. Scary beyond belief. Also a little scary for a new relationship that she knew this at 7:30 in the morning.

TALENTS

One of Gabrielle's deepest psychic strengths was to put people in touch with their gifts.

A few months after we met, Gabrielle moved to New Jersey so we could be together. It was an astounding decision. She was well-known on the West coast, but did not have a national reputation or following. We explored the possibility of my moving to California, but I couldn't make it work with my then law practice.

It was a test of all I had been teaching; to walk my talk and follow my feelings, even if it meant letting go of all I had worked years to build.

Goodbye to my mailing list, my Thursday morning ladies group, my three-story redwood house with the sunken tub, my roots, my people. I left California casual for the eastern edge, fog for humidity, cars for taxis, and the Golden Gate Bridge for the New Jersey Turnpike. And I never stopped to wonder if I was totally insane.

All for this man.

In some small way, this situation reversed itself when I retired from a very successful legal career. The whole context changed. I went overnight from "Who's the lady with Robert" to "Who's the guy with Gabrielle?" Best thing that ever happened to me! Actually, Gabrielle pointed out that I went from one side of my brain to the other.

More to this point, some people from California moved to New Jersey to work with her. One was a 17-year old girl who wrote a three-page letter to plead with Gabrielle to petition her father to allow her to do the same. Gabrielle read the letter and turned to me and said: "This little teenage girl is going to be a major writer someday." She stayed with us for three years, working in the Mirrors theater company. She returned to California and, thirty years later, became one of the highest grossing female screenwriters in the history of Hollywood.

———————————

On my first birthday we were together, Gabrielle gave me a small African hand drum. I had never seen anything like it before, but it fell into my lap like it had always been there. Thirty-five years later, my drumming has been at the bottom of 16 albums and hundreds of dance events, theater performances, workshops and classes. I've suffered from arthritis and rotator cuff problems for the last 10 years or so, but could always play drums for 2-3 hours at a time, even when I couldn't tie my shoes. But the pain has become so intense lately that I have had to give up drumming (except for Bertha). As it happens, the last time I was able to play was at Gabrielle's memorial in January 2013. Appropriate, I guess. I think I've lost the will and inspiration to push through the pain.

On our first Christmas together, she had a friend buy me an expensive, complicated (to me) Nikon camera. I had never taken a photograph in my life and was totally intimidated by this machine. I didn't touch it for 6 months and, when I finally picked it up, I broke the automatic function immediately. It was the best thing that could have happened. I became fascinated by process of putting light on film (yes, film – it was the '80's) and photography became the theme of my inner life. Turns out I had a talent for it, shot professionally for magazines and stock and sold some prints at an exhibit in the artsy world of Soho. All of the photographs in this book are mine, except where otherwise credited.[3]

She inspired a whole side of my brain that was asleep during my travels through the linear world.

HER BODY

Gabrielle was deeply and psychically connected to her body. It didn't start out that way for her. Her biggest struggle growing up was to inhabit her body. It might have had something to do with her Catholic schooling, or the general tenor of the '40's-'50's, but, as she would later say, the child/teen Gabrielle thought her body was her enemy, something to overcome or deny. She would eventually describe this as the major psychic wound of our times, "the divorce of spirit from flesh."

It took thousands of dances and rivers of sweat to bring her to the place where she could say: "My body is the spirit's wife." And occupy that body she did! She not only danced with it; she communicated with it. To watch her speak to you was just as important as to listen to her speak to you. Her connection to her body was what made her embrace so special;

<hr>

[3] I have no recent photographs. I stopped shooting after eye surgery in the early '90's.

her hug was a moment of total presence and total surrender. No bells and whistles or fireworks, but her surrender to the physical contact left you knowing that some part of your soul met some part of her soul.

And she developed an uncanny sense of what was going on in her body – its needs, equilibrium and problems. She actively guided the decisions and protocols of her 3 and ½ year cancer treatment, at times in conflict with those treating her. She came under the care of a prominent doctor at a prominent New York hospital and, as she ran out of options, eventually agreed to his prescription of a "mild" form of chemotherapy. It was comprised of two substances, both with side effects, one with the propensity to cause internal bleeding. One day, after several months of this treatment, she arrived at her appointment and told the nurses that, on this day, she would take the first substance but not the second. It didn't feel right, she told them. The nurses were flummoxed – they had never been presented with this from a patient. The doctor was called in and told Gabrielle that the use of both drugs was "not negotiable."

She acceded to his position. The first drip went well, but fifteen minutes into the second drip, all of the blood vessels in her nose exploded. She was rushed by ambulance from the doctor's office to the emergency room and it took a hospital stay of five days to get the bleeding under control. I had to beg her to forgive herself for not following her intuition.

In a subsequent visit to the doctor, he told her: "You've not only changed my life and practice, but also the lives of my patients. I will never again casually dismiss anything a patient offers with respect to her care."

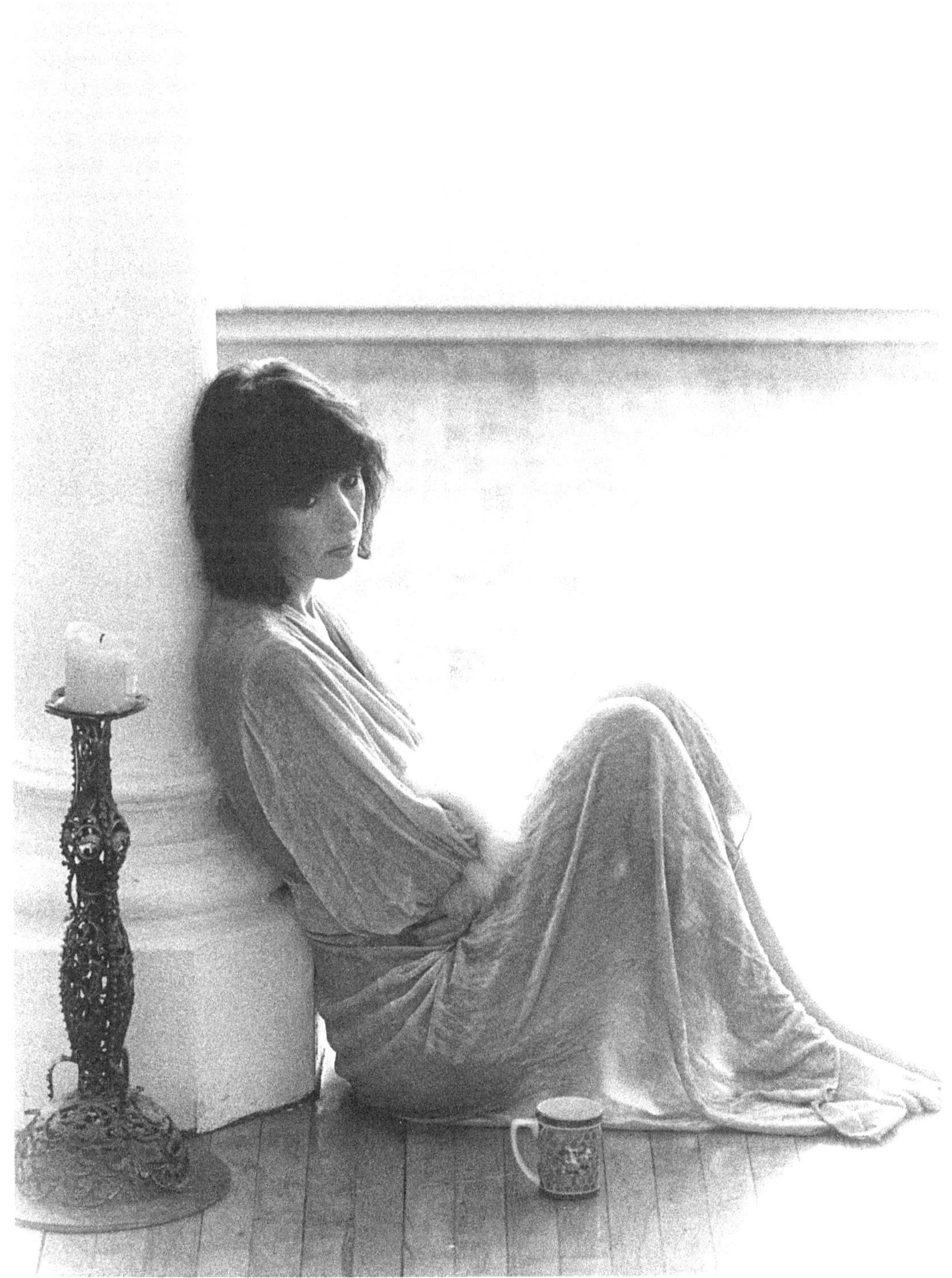

A DIRECTOR

Gabrielle was called many things. A "dancer" (she hated that), a "movement innovator" (that was OK), one of today's top 10 "Fitness Gurus", "high priestess of trance", "European rave queen", "international icon", "revered wellness-movement figure", "movement artist and trance-dance diva", "pioneer in the development of 'ecstatic dance'", "Goddess of Rhythm", "trance-dance diva", "reigning priestess of trance dance", "high priestess of trip-hop" and several forms of shaman: "highly respected New Age shaman", "aural harlot and sensuous shaman", "rock and roll shaman", "urban shaman". She flirted with "shaman" and we even used it one year for an announcement of her teaching schedule – *The Shaman Hits the Road*. We used an official NJ license plate I got as a joke gift for her birthday.

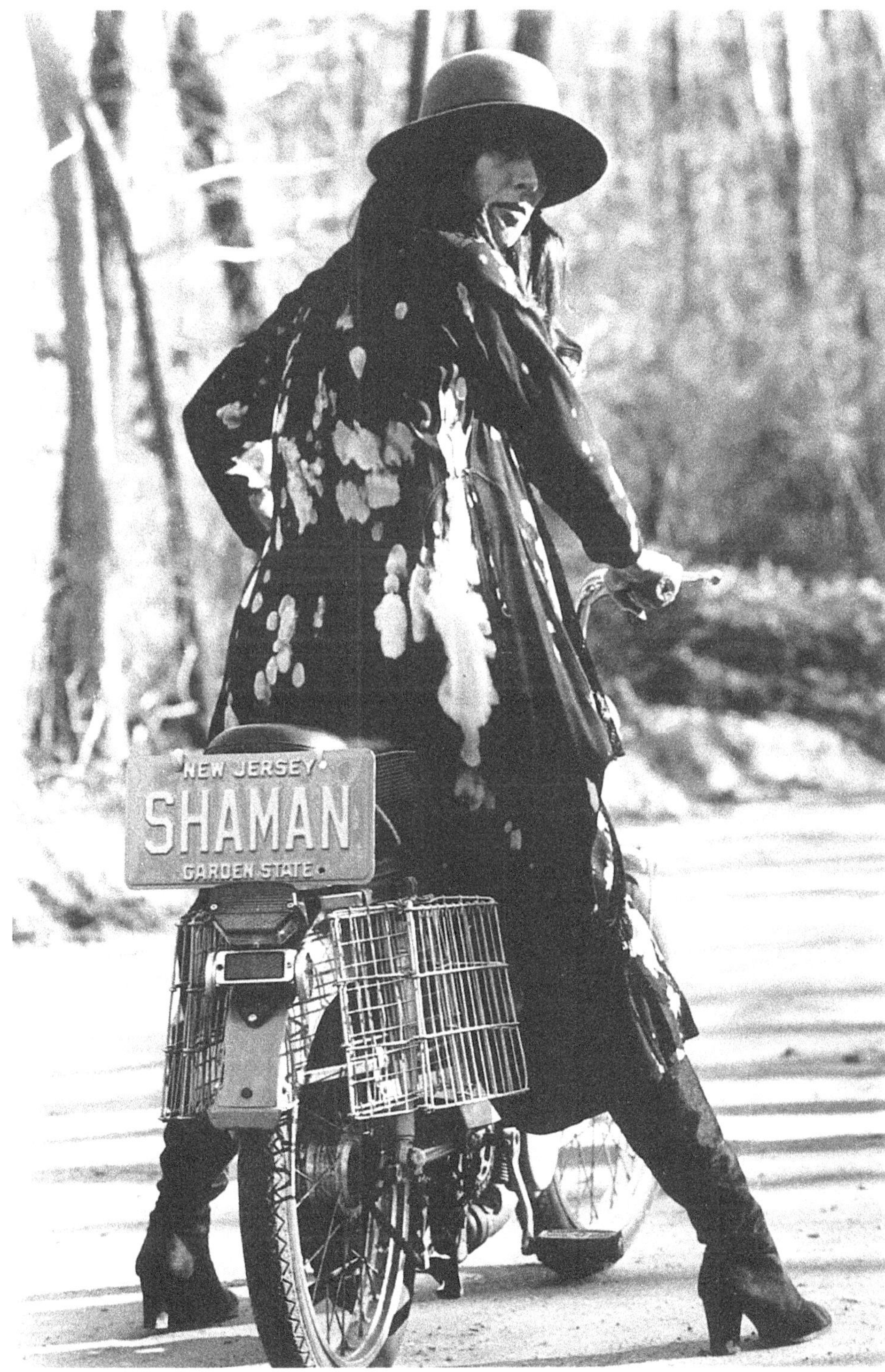

Gabrielle started to take it seriously when the brilliant anthropologist, Gregory Bateson, asked her to teach a workshop with him called "The Shaman and the Anthropologist." They adored each other – I used to call them G². The only time Gabrielle told me she was intimidated in a teaching context was when, at the beginning of a workshop at Esalen, she looked up to find Gregory *mofo* Bateson sitting in front of her as a student. I found out later he used to take a lot of crap from the big-shot male teachers at Esalen – they would challenge him for being in her classes and workshops. Gregory's response was: "When that lady talks, I listen!" We visited him in the hospital during the last week of his life. As we left his room, he called her over and whispered: "I don't think I'll be dancing with you anymore, Gabrielle!"

THEATER/WORKSHOPS

At bottom, she was a director. She loved to guide process—artistic process and healing process. Viewed from an overall perspective, her events were theatrical performances even though they were billed as movement experiences. I saw her direct 2000 people one night in a hotel ballroom who thought they were there for a dance event.

What she did in workshops belongs in the theater category because that is what it was. There were dancing and writing and meditative exercises, but it was when people expressed themselves in theatrical, physical form that was the payoff. Physical – for Gabrielle, it didn't count if it couldn't be embodied.

She called this Ritual Theater, and it was her favorite part of "teaching". The exercise was to embody (alone or in groups) the various rhythms, feelings, and issues that were the subject of the workshop, using words if necessary, but expressing the physicality of it. The performances that people did for each other in workshops were like Tibetan sand paintings – if you were there, you saw them, but they blew away when the workshop ended.

She often complained that her healing work continuously took over the time she wanted to devote more formally to her theater work. It was hard for her to say "no" to the demands of her teaching schedule and the needs of those who wanted to do 5Rhythms workshops.

There were three "formal" phases of her theater work[4]. The first was in New Jersey. After those 9 or 10 people moved East to work with her, she formed them into a theater company and band, The Mirrors. I was part of it, having given up my law practice by then. The theater work was basically about rhythm and the ego. We had a studio in Red Bank and worked there daily. During the week, we would strip our psyches bare to find the patterns that disconnected us from our power and possibilities. We would perform the results on the weekends, in the studio and eventually venues in San Francisco, New York, Philadelphia and Washington, D.C. I used to call it a psychic peep show.

Gabrielle guided us in the exploration of our egos, the structure and patterns of our psyches we place between our vulnerable essence and the world "out there". She developed a piece for me based on the part of my ego that feeds on resentment. We called him Sidney Sniper. He would slink around the stage in sniper firing positions and announce: "I never waste my anger in the moment. I like to hold on to it and lie in wait until I can really hurt someone with it."

---

[4] She also directed some works by others, including Sam Sheperd/Joseph Chaikin's SAVAGE LOVE, starring Jonny and Lorca and a piece for the One-Act Theater Festival in NYC. She was also a member of the Playright & Director's Unit of the Actors Studio.

Late one night, during these New Jersey days, we got a phone call from one of the cast who, in one of life's sweet anomalies, had to go-go dance to earn the money to pay for her spiritual training. She was at a pay phone outside of a bar in Springfield MA, sobbing with humiliation at her circumstances. "This is great, sweetheart," Gabrielle said. "Dance that pain, spend that energy and make sure that you take notes of everything you are feeling and saying. This is going to make great theater!"

It was a little difficult for me to perform because I couldn't sing, dance or act well enough to interest anyone. There was also a physician and the others were mostly singers and musicians. But the work was so raw and pure and essential and powerful that a Tony-winning Broadway producer came to New Jersey, saw a performance at our studio and began to negotiate with me and Gabrielle about a legitimate run. We even began the casting process with an audition for 350 actors-singers-dancers. Gabrielle ended the negotiations when the producer suggested casting Olivia Newton-John in the lead role as the shaman.

These are photos of members of the original Mirrors theater group in the NJ days.

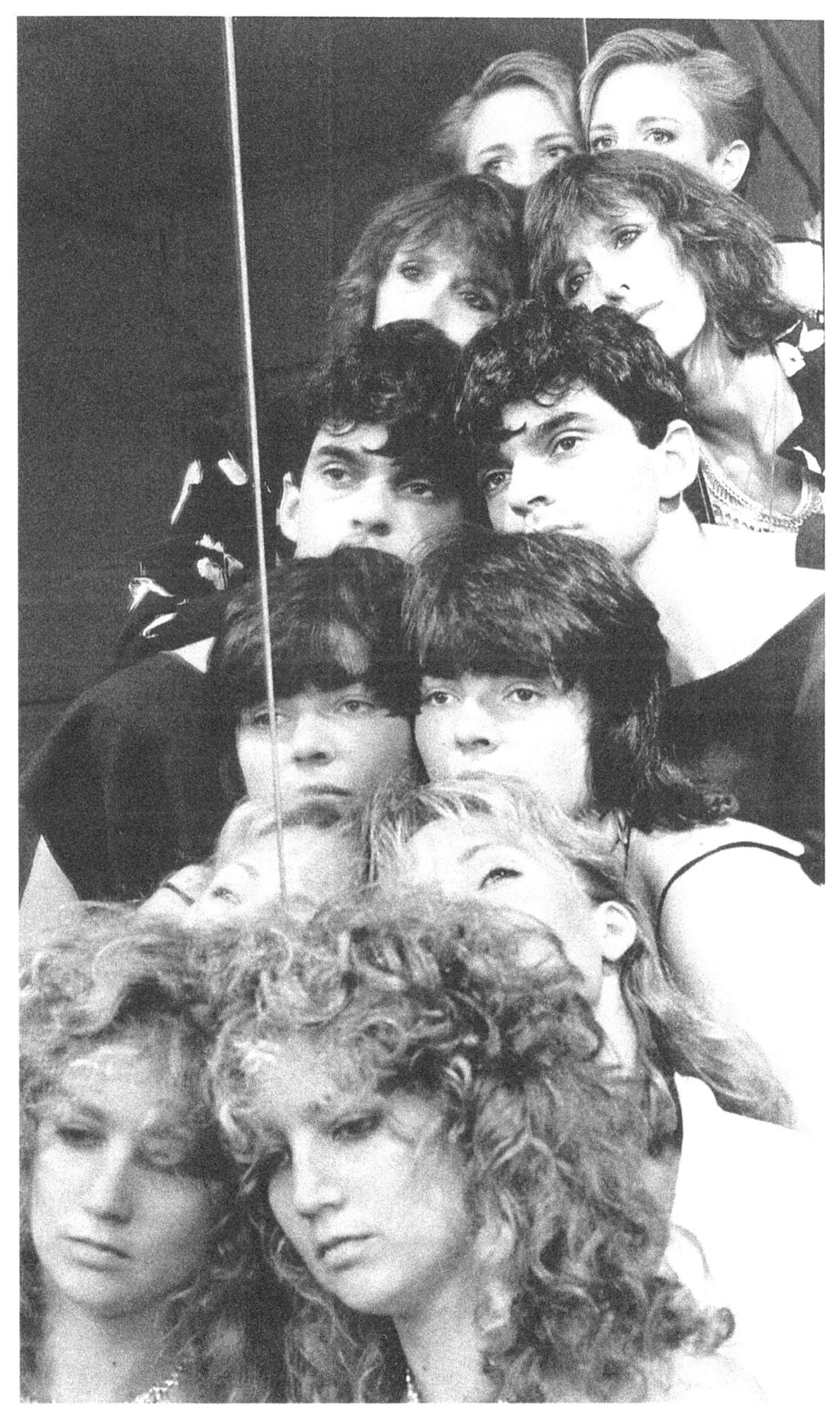

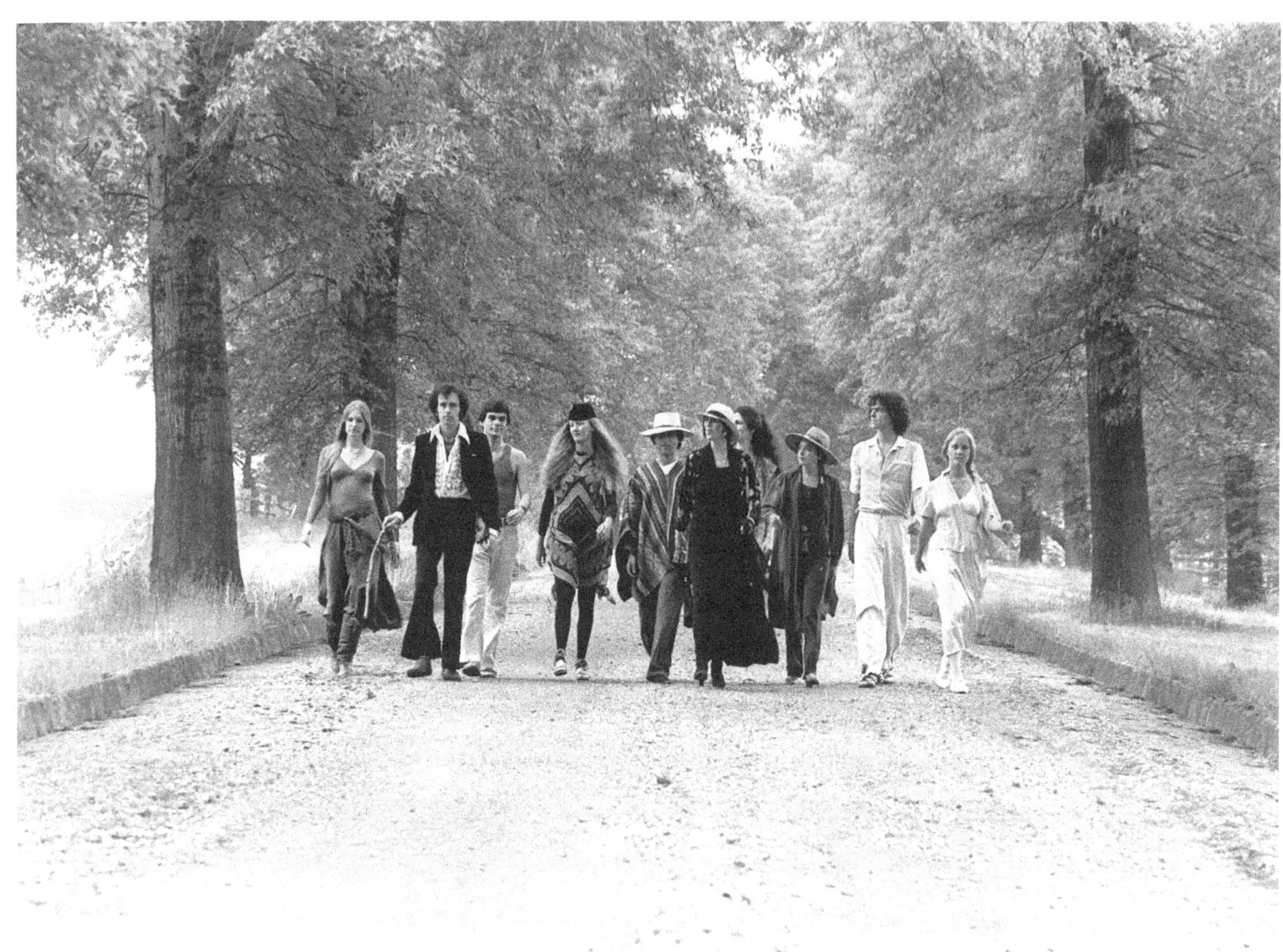

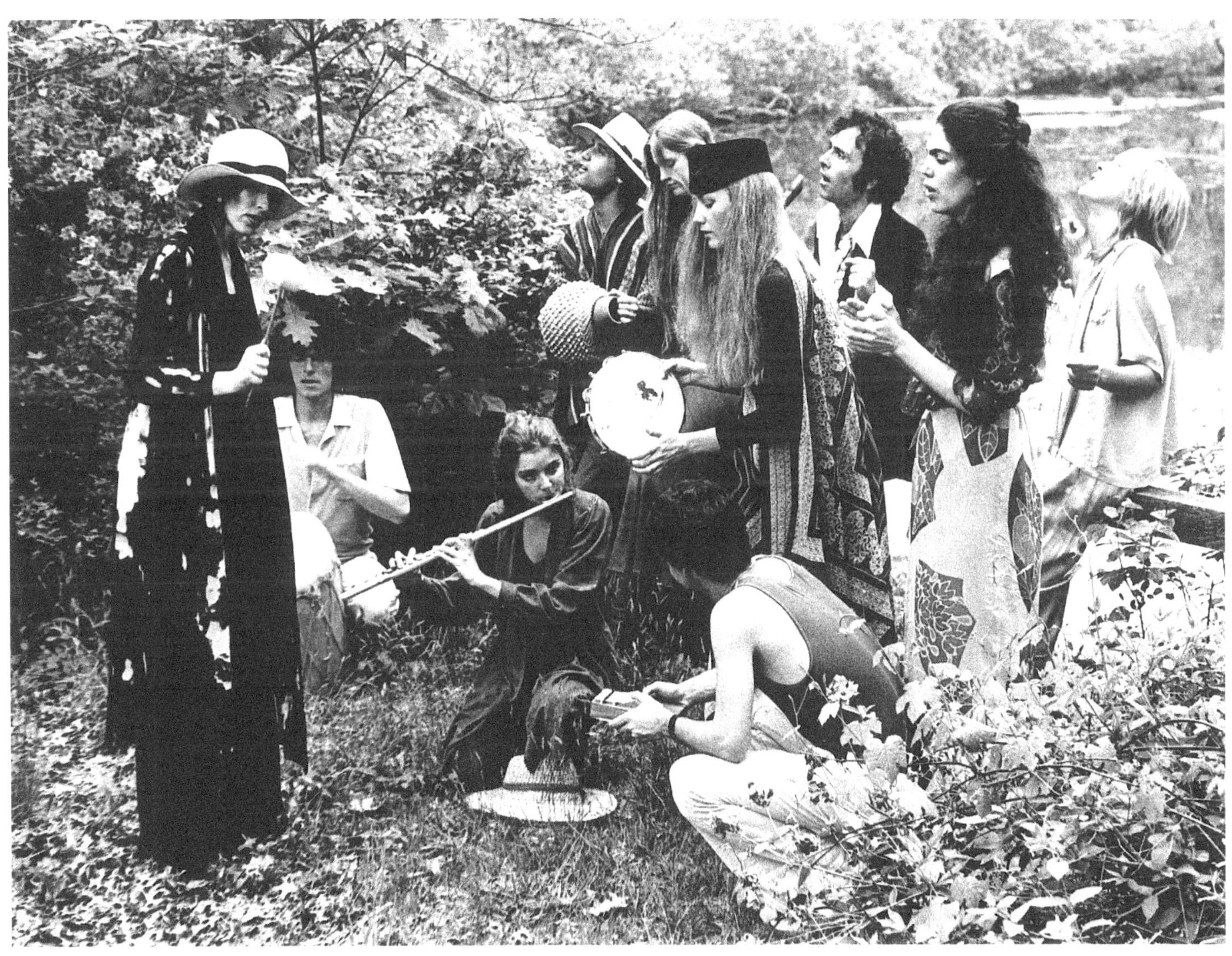

The second presentation was more about dance than theater. She was hired to direct a piece for the opening of a huge club in Chelsea, one of those trendy, celebrity-driven, bottle-selling, go-to venues that dot the New York night landscape. She actually choreographed the dancers and included aerialists and jugglers. I called it "Cirque de Ga-Bay". It was performed on 6 successive Saturday nights, from 10:00 PM to 6:00 AM. I barely survived the 8 straight hours of pounding club music, not to mention the one night when 250 drunken people dressed as Santa Claus (from that *Santacon* phenomenon) comprised most of the audience.

The most wonderful thing to come out of this was Nilaya, an extraordinary being who auditioned and was hired for the show. She is a 5'2" dynamo with the appetite of a bus driver and the power and grace of a traditional (Indian), modern and ecstatic dancer. She and Gabrielle connected deeply and, after the run of the show, Nil began to come to our home. It seemed social at first, but it turned out that she had a brilliant mind (economics major at Wesleyan), could type as fast as Gabrielle could talk, and was so in tune with Gabrielle and her thinking that she soon took over as Gabrielle's assistant and editor, positions that were sorely needed and difficult to fill.

Gabrielle really needed this help on a daily basis – there was an entire 5Rhythms world that required more than she had to give alone. I did what I could to help, but the demands were bigger than both of us. They worked together effortlessly and seamlessly, one concerted, unified, loving team.

All was well until Cirque du Soleil stole Nilaya right out from under us and she went off to Europe for 2 years. Keeping up with everything was difficult for Gabrielle during that time, but then the Cirque gig ended and Nil was back. Briefly, unfortunately, because then Madonna hired this dynamic talent and off she went on tour again – this time, for a year and a half.

By the end of the Madonna tour, Gabrielle had been diagnosed with cancer and, when Nil returned, she showed up at our home to offer herself in total service – whatever was necessary, at any time, for no compensation (we didn't let that last long). So our dear Nilaya became totally and wonderfully enmeshed in our lives as an assistant, colleague, nurse, editor, daughter, friend, student and teacher. She even modeled for the cover of our album *Jhoom*. She and Ruthie (Gabrielle's masseuse, aroma-therapist, herbologist, essential oilist and all around delightful, loving and nutty caregiver) and Lekha (a dearest friend, philanthropist, filmmaker and all-around amazing person) became the most loving support system that carried Gabrielle and me to the end. We were so blessed.

The third formal theater process came toward the end. It was an astounding blessing. Lekha decided to fund and produce a documentary of Gabrielle's life and work, and a portion of it was devoted to giving Gabrielle the opportunity (time and funding) to develop, rehearse and perform a ritual theater piece. This was thrilling to her – as sick as she was, she could focus on theater! There was a two-week workshop with acting and musical artists to develop the piece and it was eventually presented to the public at PS122, a noted, experimental theater venue in NYC. It was called *Sole to Soul*. Although her cancer was ravaging her by that point, Gabrielle pulled it off. She would come home each night drained and delighted. The exhilaration of the process and the opportunity to devote herself to theater made the pain bearable for her. She was so happy!

MUSIC

Because we used her name in the title of the band (who was going to buy music from Robert Ansell & The Mirrors?), many people thought Gabrielle was a musician. She wasn't. She was a director. Always a director. I pulled the lead oar in the making of the music, but she was the guide and catalyst.

Almost all of our albums began with bottom drum tracks I put down, often with Sanga of the Valley, often alone. I am a bottom drummer, the lowest in the musical food chain of the lowest in the musical food chain. Since I was at the bottom of the music, I realized that I should concentrate on the bottom of the people dancing in the room. Yup – I got the feet and Sanga got all the good parts. I must have been a podiatrist in my last life. Sanga tells a story about me that I'm not sure is true. "Did you see that gorgeous woman dancing in the room," he supposedly asked me. "I'm not sure", I supposedly said. "What did her feet look like?"

My job was to create the foundation of an energy that Gabrielle needed in the moment to help the dancers get to where she wanted to help them go. If some beats or patterns I made up worked, if they got people moving, I remembered and eventually recorded them. Actually, to be honest, I not only watched the feet, but also Gabrielle's butt. For more than thirty years, I watched Gabrielle's butt. That was the guide post. If that thing was moving, we were grooving. If it wasn't, we weren't. Simple!

Gabrielle and I built the songs from these butt-moving bottoms up, deciding what bass player to add to the drums, what vocalist, or violinist, etc. We managed to get astounding musicians to play with us, maybe because of the freedom we gave them, maybe because of the chance to work with Gabrielle. Her actual studio participation varied from album to album; for some, she was at most of the sessions; for some, she came when we needed her to get a specific performance from a musician; for some, she was only at the mixes. And, a lot of our work came outside the studio, at home, listening to the tracks and deciding how to bring them to the next level. She didn't always know what would work, but she always knew what didn't.

It started with the album, *Dancing Toward the One*, back in the days when we were a rock 'n' roll band. Gabrielle wanted an uninterrupted wave through the 5 rhythms, 5 minutes of each. We were going live – 24 recording tracks, 25 minutes, 6 musicians and 3 vocalists. This was a prodigious undertaking. We all worked on this for a week or two prior to the recording session, and developed and rehearsed charts to pull this off. Five minutes before we started to record, Gabrielle walked into the studio, tore up the charts and told us she would dance while we recorded. "Play me," she said. We did.

Rock 'n' roll was great, but Gabrielle's spirit was more primitive and tribal. I guess I was responsible for our move to ambient music. Gabrielle loved to use live drums in her classes and workshops. In 1979 and '80, she was teaching a weekly class in New York City, and I was playing drums with Gordy (a dear friend and member of the Baba Olatunji band) and an elderly (late '60's) Cuban percussionist, Manuel, I had seen playing in Central Park. We were playing wonderful rhythms and the people were dancing intensely to them. I thought it would be a good idea to record the "bottoms" we were coming up with weekly. We added pitch instruments to them and they became our first major album, *Totem*, a (then) new style of music for dancing and ambience – no lyrics, no choruses, no verses – a rhythm ride. Great for dancing; great for making love. Gabrielle and I always did a test drive.

I was a little concerned at this session because Manuel would occasionally break into song when we were playing at the classes. He spoke almost no English. I can get by in Spanish, but not with anyone from Cuba; their speed and accent floor me. Before the engineer hit RECORD, I turned to Manuel and said "No cantele" or something like that. We were going three drummers at a time, money was tight and I didn't want to waste a take. Sure enough, several minutes into the song, Manuel started singing. The engineer looked at me through the glass, but I shook my head so he would keep recording. It turned out great – in fact, we called the song *La Cancion de Manuel*. To this day, I'm not really sure what the words were. When we asked him, all we could get was that he was singing about the "ritual". Gabrielle had been dancing in the control room while we were recording and he could see her through the glass.

Of course, after making this music, it was my job to sell it. Not an easy task. We were "bin-challenged." There were very few bins in those days. We weren't rock, we weren't soul, we weren't jazz, we weren't classical, we weren't pop. What to do? Gabrielle's movement work was moving through this milieu called "New Age" and I thought I could get some distribution in that market which was just emerging. Not! It turned out that New Age music in those days was all harps, feathers, synthesizers and balloons. Our music had drums, and drums were not spiritual in the early '80's. But we pushed on and, eventually our music found its way around the globe. And drums are now happening!

I had working titles for all of the songs as we went along with each album. None of them lasted. Gabrielle handled the titles for our songs, sometimes to capture the essence of a completed song, sometimes to guide the development of one. The album *Bones* is a good example. I had put down six bottoms, basic drums only and sent a cassette to Gabrielle who was teaching in Europe for a long stretch. A week later, we're on the phone and she says: "Not sure what we'll call this album, but bottom #3 should be a warm-up and we'll make the other five songs in the rhythms, but call them by the name of animals. And she named the animals." Hence, the album *Bones*, with its songs *Dolphin* (flowing), *Raven* (staccato), *Snake* (chaos), *Deer* (lyrical) and *Wolf* (stillness). And she pulled another one of her G-strings for the song, *Snake*. We decided we wanted a violin over the drums. Gabrielle said it had to be a mournful violinist. Three days later, we walked into our favorite coffee shop and ran into our friend Boris, the Russian rock 'n' roll idol who we later made the albums, *Refuge* and *Bardo* with. He was excited to introduce us to a new friend, Jonny Cunningham, at the next table. He happened to be a violin player in a popular rock band. A Scottish violin player. The archetypical mournful violin player.

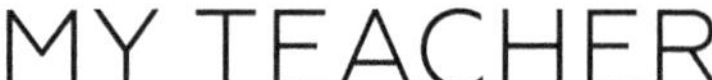

MY TEACHER

Literally.

When we fell in love, I had no idea what she did for a living. When she told me, I still had no idea what she did for a living. I was a lawyer from New Jersey. I knew nothing about rhythms, ecstasy, movement or shamans.

I resisted for a while. But, after living together for 6 months, I agreed to go to Esalen Institute to attend a workshop she was doing there and see what this was all about. It was a weekend workshop and, after the Friday night session, we went to the hot tubs – my first experience of "public" nudity (I discovered that people are generally more attractive with some clothes on). I was in the shower when the naked lady next to me said: "Are you here with Gabrielle?" "Yes", I said. "Too bad", she replied." I really wanted to fuck you." Welcome to Esalen! And, in spite of or maybe because of the attitude under that exchange, I grew to love Esalen and spent many wonderful times working there over the years.

I was a student in the room when she started her theater work in NJ. I did all the exercises with my wife as my teacher and director. I also did the exercises in classes and workshops when I wasn't drumming. I think it's a tribute to both of us that it wasn't a problem for us, or the others in the room.

I backed off as time went by. It was more important that I play drums and oversee the productions and probably even more important that I was available to give Gabrielle a voice and an ear that had some distance from the process that was going on in the room. In creating that distance from the participants, I became an outside resource, a father figure. Strange – all I ever wanted in life was to be a sex symbol, but I kept turning out to be a father figure.

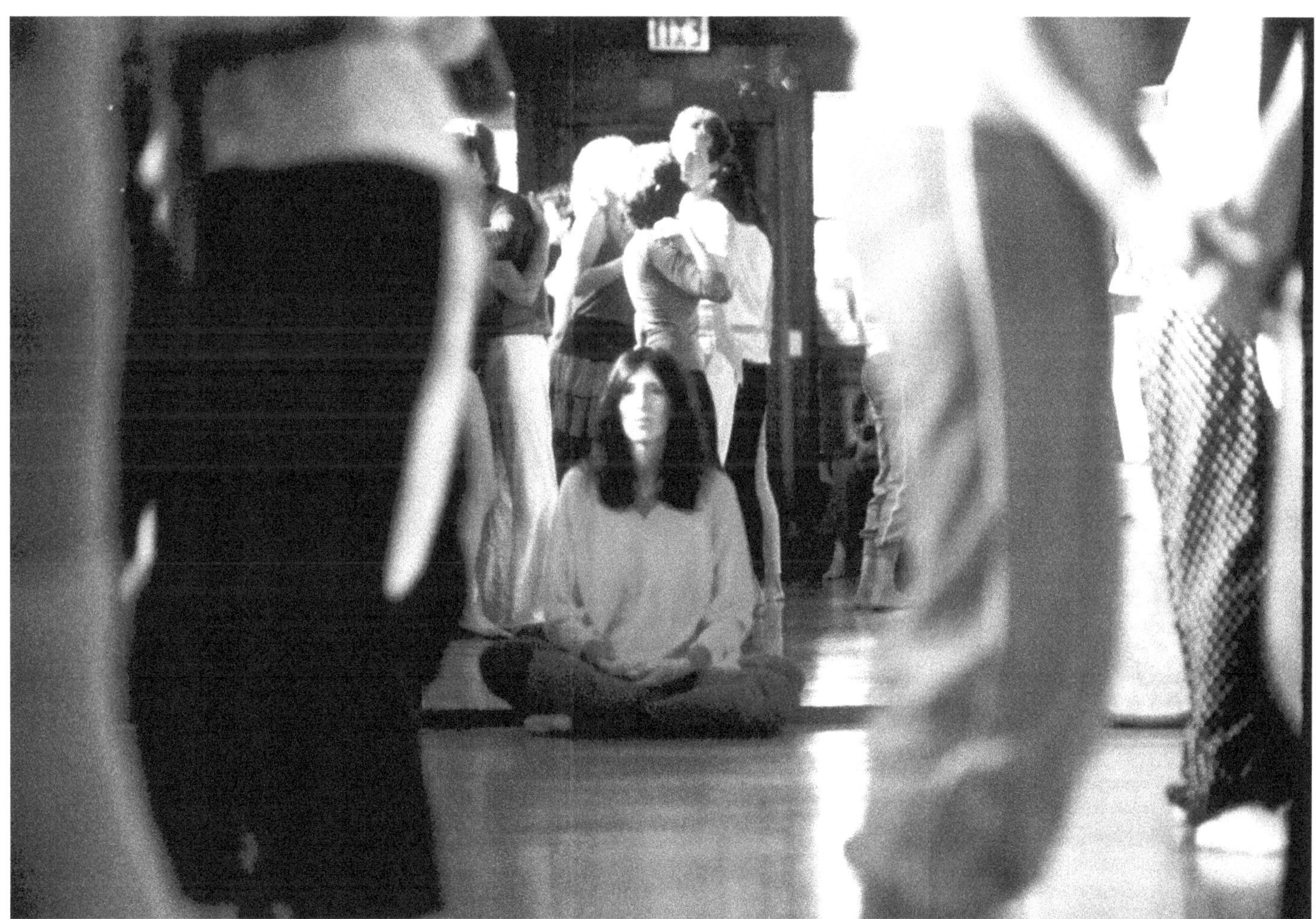

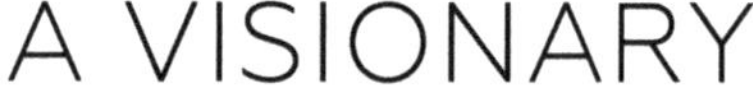

A VISIONARY

Gabrielle did not set out to be a visionary. She didn't have a plan to conquer the world. In fact, it was only a few years before she died that she began to think seriously about a plan to organize and structure the body of work she had created. And that was more about having something concrete to pass on to her son, Jonathan, than to secure her place in history.

Life was always about the moment for her. The moment and movement – movement of the body. As she said many times: "The body is the Bible."

She was deeply committed to attacking what she considered our deepest cultural wound, the divorce of spirit from flesh, something for which we can thank all of our major religions. She taught that "spiritual" didn't mean anything if it wasn't embodied. As she put it, "My body is my spirit's wife." That was the marriage made in heaven. And, of course, for Gabrielle, the easiest, most effective, dramatic and creative way to be physical was to dance.

She was not alone in looking at dance as something other than an art form. Anna Halprin and Emilie Conrad were mining a similar lode. But Gabrielle's insistence on the physicality of any useful psychological healing process was singular, especially her commitment to seeing energy as its basic component, rhythm. "Rhythm is our mother tongue," she would say, and she saw it in people's personas, movements, eating habits, closets, lovers, residences, families and more.

She was deeply connected to Esalen Institute in Big Sur, California. She lived there in the late '60's-early '70's, gave birth to Jonny there and worked there, on and off, for most of her adult life.

This connection guaranteed that she would be present for much of the innovative, human potential philosophies, practices and programs that were developing at that time and changing the landscape of personal healing and growth. It was all intellectual work, driven by the mind, confined to the mind, disdainful of the body.

When Gabrielle was developing her 5Rhythms work, the body was not the medium for any important, transformative, healing modalities. It was all about the head and thinking and musing and processing and writing and speaking – in other words, words. Gabrielle had no problem with words; she wrote three books, after all. It's just that they were not enough for her by themselves.

It took the ultimate rebel, Fritz Perls, to help break the mold. He was exploring and teaching his Gestalt therapy model at Esalen when he met Gabrielle. Fascinated (who wouldn't be?), he eventually asked her to come to his groups and lead his students in her movement exercises – help them move their bodies! This was groundbreaking and led to many other opportunities for her. She told me once that Fritz had seen her coming up the path from the Esalen baths and she was reading one of his books. He tore the book from her hands, threw it into the Pacific Ocean and told her that, if he knew what she knew, he would never have written that book!

Even without the psychological/healing underpinnings and overlay of her 5Rhythms work, Gabrielle was instrumental in making movement/dance relevant, popular, hip and important. Around the globe! So, today we have NIA, Ecstatic Dance Programs, Open Floor, Soul Motion, Movement Medicine, and a host of "conscious dance" practices (even a magazine by that name). Most of these were created by her students, some by students of her students, some independently. But they all owe a debt of gratitude to Gabrielle and her dancing feet and mind.

She was the first, she was the most dynamic, she was the most influential and, with apologies to Anna and Emilie, she was the most gorgeous!

She had been dancing alone in our studio in NJ and was in "the zone" when she came up for air. I had bought those earrings for her early in our relationship – one of those times when you know you made a good choice. She loved them. After she passed, I gave them to a rock 'n roll friend who was very dear to her. It was important to me that they stayed "in the family."

About one year before she died, Gabrielle told me that this was her favorite picture ever taken of her. I was so impressed with myself that it was hard for me to be around me for a few days. I can't believe it took her 34 frickin' years to tell me how much she loved this photo. Everything changes when you are diagnosed with cancer.

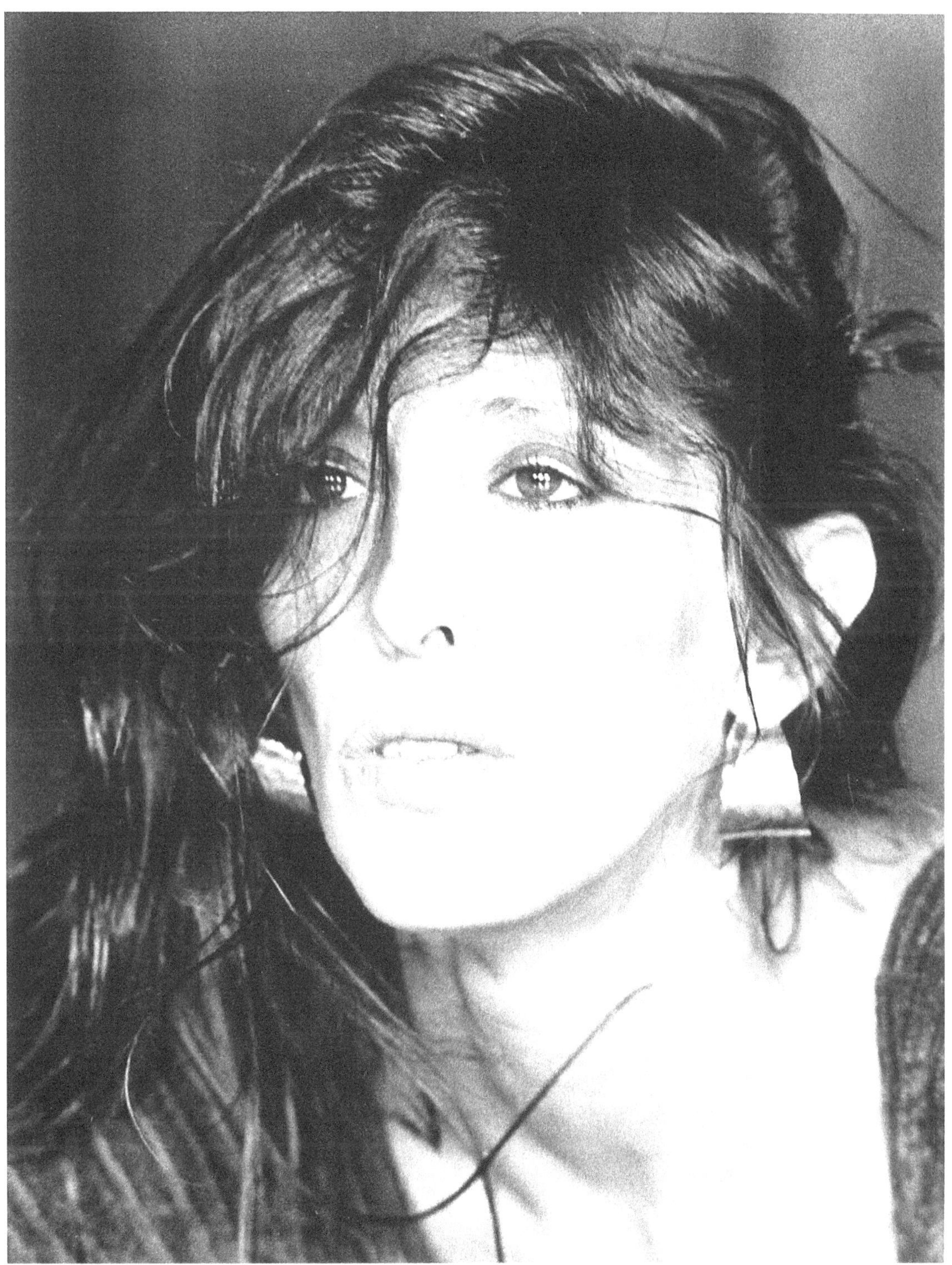

UNIQUE

Gabrielle was unique in her style, unique in her mixture of the sacred and profane in her teaching, unique in her form of dancing, unique in her family. Of course, she'd stand out in any family not named Addams. She could walk into a room and galvanize it by her presence alone. But, she never demanded attention for her specialness, for being who she was. I cannot recall a single occasion where she wanted, needed or demanded attention that was not required by a teaching, directing or performing situation. Being Gabrielle, she could just as readily do the opposite and disappear in a crowd. She loved just being another body in a yoga class, even though the yoga teacher may have been an adoring fan and the other students would have been thrilled to know that she was in the room.

She would laugh at my referring to her as "unique". She thought everyone was, if they would only be true to themselves. For her, uniqueness was an essential part of the human condition and the central theme of all of her teaching and theater work.

It agonized her to see people trapped as "nice, normal, neutral neurotics." And, she never did anything because "that's the way it's done." Such thinking was only an impetus for her to bring her uniqueness to whatever was being done. One of her students pointed out that the difference between Gabrielle and Sigmund Freud is that Freud determined one's mental health by how tightly one could hold it all together, while Gabrielle determined mental health by how easily one could let it all fall apart. I was reminded of that recently when Nilaya and I were having dinner in an upscale restaurant and she was telling me one of her incredible G stories. It hit a nerve and I started crying at the table – sobbing, actually. Nilaya made absolutely no move to stop me, a total Gabrielle reaction. She would no more say to someone "Don't cry", than she would say "Don't breathe." Crying was just a dance to her, another way for the body to let go of something. As long as there was a reason for it.

Her devotion to her uniqueness did, on occasion, lead to difficulty. It was never easy for her to toe the company line. Her deepest spiritual training was with Oscar Ichazo and his Arica school in the early '70's. It was extremely important to her, but it was a "school"; it had a program and rules and formalities. Not surprisingly, she was thrown out of the school after a while. Those that ran it could not handle her independence (which I believe translates to breaking the rules). Shortly after her eviction, Ichazo himself called her to say that he wanted to work with her privately and individually. Maybe his school couldn't put up with her, but he sure could and did.

MAMA G

I was asked about how people came to call Gabrielle "Mama G". Was it a guru thing? Of course, there was no one on the planet further from guru consciousness than Gabrielle, so here's how it came about.

It started with Ruthie. She worked with Gabrielle for years and would rub and cradle her while murmuring "Baby G" or telling me not to worry – she was taking good care of Baby G. I thought that was fun and started to call her Lady G (even Your G-ness) in emails, texts and conversations. Soon, our daughters-in-law, Amber and Sara, picked up the theme with Mama G, as did Nilaya (who later was the first person to shorten it to just G). And, the "G" stuck. Our grandchildren, Sofia and Luke, started calling her Nana G. Mama G started to find its way to the 5Rhythms teachers around the globe as a term of affection and came into regular usage. Gabrielle never objected. I think she actually once signed an email to them as Mama G. She was so protective of them and could become a "mama grizzly" if any of them were ever threatened.

I guess I cemented the G-osity when I got the letter "G" tattooed in the crook between my left thumb and forefinger, probably the most romantic thing I've ever done. I became insecure for Gabrielle after her cancer diagnosis (a total projection and probably unnecessary). I put myself in her shoes and wondered what I would be afraid of (other than dying and death, of course) if I were in her position. The first thing that came to me was the fear of losing the love of my life to the future, the fear that she would realize that her time with me was limited and would leave the present (psychologically) to plan a future without me. A switch would be tripped. That would be unbearable and I determined that no such thought about me should cloud her healing or dying path.

My solution to this came a few months into the 3 and ½ year cancer process. Gabrielle went to Germany with Ruthie for 10 days to get some up-to-date holistic and orthodox diagnosis and treatment. I decided to have a remarriage/recommitment ceremony for the benefit of both of us and thought that branding myself with a "G" would do the trick. I took her signature (from a check, actually) to the tattoo parlor and had the artist copy her G, which looks a little like the infinity sign. I emailed her this photo and, although I am probably the first man ever to do a remarriage/recommitment ritual without his wife, Ruthie told me that Gabrielle was thrilled and giggled and sighed at my gesture. Giggling and sighing are good after 30+ years.

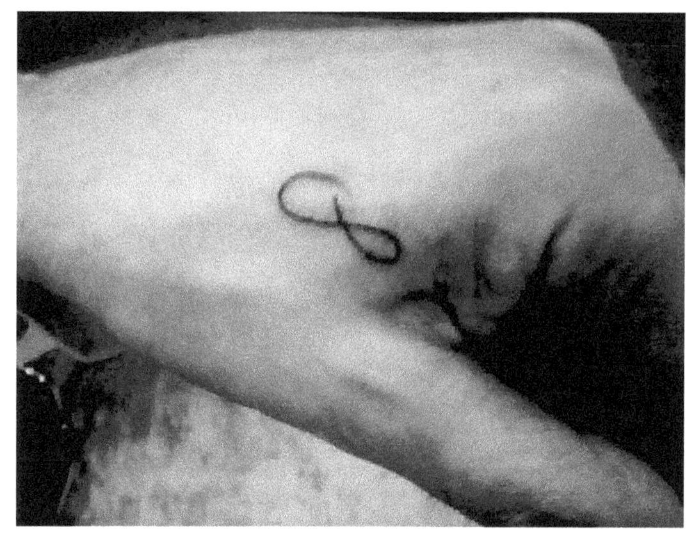

Photo by Arthur Retiz, Jr.

I call it my G-spot.

A couple of months later, Gabrielle and Ruthie had to go back to Germany. I bought a stencil and some water-soluble markers and had Arthur, our office manager, do this:

Photo by Arthur Retiz, Jr.

I sent the photo to Germany with the question: "Do you think I went too far this time?"

So, the beat goes on. I recently moved from our home of 35 years to a new co-op down the block. It was time. My apartment number is now 4G – for G.

Can you believe it? She's still messing with me.

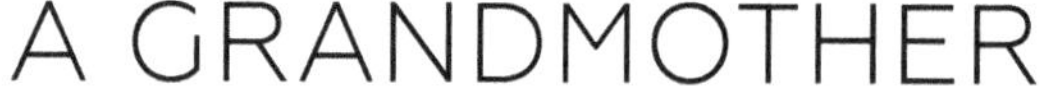

A GRANDMOTHER

It was impossible to be around Gabrielle and not find inspiration in one form or other. It didn't matter how old or young you were. I love this email exchange between her and our granddaughter, Sofia, who was 11 years old at the time. It all started so simply with "Hi Nana":

On Nov 4, 2011, at 6:38 PM, sofia ansell wrote:

hi nana

wolves :)

On Sat, Nov 5, 2011 at 1:47 PM, Gabrielle Roth <gabraven@panix.com> wrote:

hi sofia,

i love wolves.

silver ones.

i love their song and the way they move together.

i love that they mate for life like ravens.

i love you,

nana

On Nov 12, 2011, at 11:28 AM, sofia ansell wrote:

dear nana,

i do too that is a great like saying did you make that up?

i love you nana,

sofia<328.png>

On Sat, Nov 12, 2011 at 4:58 PM, Gabrielle Roth <gabraven@panix.com> wrote:

yes i made it up. it's me talking to you.

i like dogs too.

especially german shepherds.

i wish i had a black one and a white one.

i would call them raven and snow.

they would go with me everywhere

even in my dreams.

love you,

nana

From: Sofia Ansell <pandaansell@gmail.com>

Date: November 12, 2011 7:29:22 PM EST

To: Gabrielle Roth <gabraven@panix.com>

Subject: Re: Re:

that is sooo awesome but the only issue with a german shepard is there is not enough room in you house!!!

love you,

sofia :)

On Sat, Nov 12, 2011 at 6:31 PM, Gabrielle Roth <gabraven@panix.com> wrote:

and that's why they only exist in my heart.

they can dance there to my beat and nobody has

to take them for a walk or a run which they prefer.

a girl can dream.

can't she?

love,

nana g

From: Sofia Ansell <pandaansell@gmail.com>

Date: November 13, 2011 11:48:14 AM EST

To: Gabrielle Roth <gabraven@panix.com>, daddy <kevansell@aol.com>

Subject: Re: Re: Re:

ok nana i understand,

 i love you sooooooooooooooooooooooooooooo much that i wrote you a short-story and here it is i watched as the wind whipped around the trees, covering the ground with snow.   mother was in the house making a concoction of different ingredients for soup.

" can i have a dog" i pleaded twisting a strand of my slick black hair around my mitten.

" NO, kainii you can not have a dog we dont have the room". my mother replied.

i sighed and looked out the window of our little wooden cottage in alaska. The ground outside was nothing but snow. i watched as the northern lights reached the mountain peaks.

" dear god, please let there be a dog out there for me someday..." i whispered. I traced the pattern of the lights on the window.

" Kainii time for dinner", mother said.

" where is dad", i asked with concern.

" your father is out there, he will be home tommorow", my mother whispered and touched her heart," i know he is safe, the spirits are taking care of him." i looked at her and smiled. " now who want's dinner" mother said lighting up her face with a smile.

after dinner i climed into the little bed in my room and fell asleep.

the next day i got into my warm clothes and my winter coat , snow boots and mittens and went outside. the snow crunched underneath my feet.

" kainii, kainii your fathers boat is back" the shopkeeper cried.

i raced home and screamed " MOTHER MOTHER, DAD IS HOME HIS BOAT IS HERE !!!!!!!!" Mother came outside in her snow suit and mittens and yelled with concern " Lets get to the docks". as mom and i were running she said " i got a phone call and your fathers boat did come but crashed and they are trying to find everyone. my face went into a state of terror and i zoomed past mother and raced to the docks. the boat was in half sitting on the shallow water. lots of town people were crowding around the dock trying to help. i pushed through all the people to find lots of workers in rafts carrying sailors back to shore.

as the first one approched i yelled " is kowichii there is my father alive?" nobody answered. tears started to swell up in my eyes as i ran into the forest and started to cry. it was always so quiet in the forest. crunch . a stick broke i opened me tear stained eyes and looked around. it could be a wolf, i thought to my self. i started to back up but i saw a blurry back figure and a white one beside it. they were coming towards me. i sat in the snow very still. I now saw them perfectly . they were german shepards. they trotted over to me and i pet them.

" do you have names." ? i asked them. i think god sent them here to help.

The white one started to roll in the snow. " i will name you snow" i cried. "i will name you raven because you are black.

" the dogs responded when i called them to come they were well trained. they both followed me everywhere. we ran to the docks and i easly found my mother. "mother, mother i cried "look god sent them" mother looked at me with a surprised look on her face the dogs sped past us and into the water.

" Raven, Snow where are you going "? i screamed.

" SHHHHHHHH" my mother put a finger in my lips. they were inside the boat now and barking rapidly. " LOOK THE DOGS ARE BARKING SOMEBODY IS STILL INSIDE " My mother screamed. "father" i whispered. people in yellow rafts were rafting inside.

after 10 minutes someone had a man on the raft he looked a little bit unconscious and i knew exactly who it was.,..... father.

the two dogs paddeled to shore and i ran up to them and gave them a hug. " you will always be in my heart" i whispered in their ear and kissed the top of each head. they began to run into the forest and was never seen again.

me and my mother brought dad home and put him on the couch then gave him wash

 clothes and tea and he woke up. we hugged him and i told him about the 2 spirit dogs that

 god sent down and saved him.

i ran to the window and there they were in the sky running through the northern lights.

" thank you " i whispered, and i touched my heart.

Gabrielle was delighted to learn that a friend was raising a wolf, one of her spirit animals.

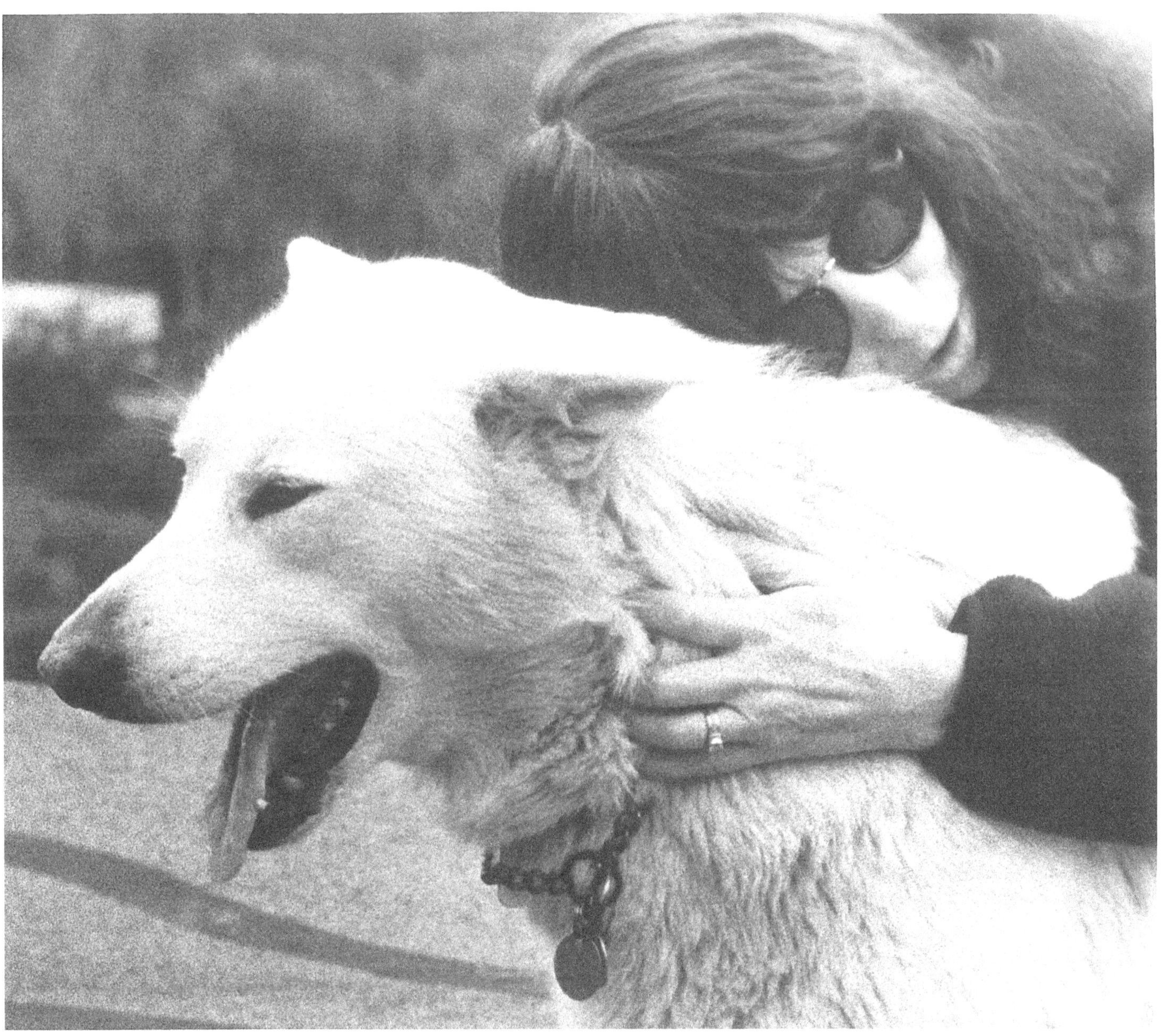

A WARRIOR

The stories of Gabrielle teaching under adverse conditions are legion, whether it was the condition of the venue (she once had to do a dance workshop in an underground parking garage in Texas) or the condition of her health (colds, flus, fevers, canker sores, broken bones, etc.). The most heartbreaking for me had to do with her cancer.

She was diagnosed on a Wednesday in early July 2009. She had been feeling pain and heaviness in her chest for a long while and it was the only time since I knew her that she did not immediately plug into her physical condition. In retrospect, it is astounding that this went on for a long time without her knowing it. She was so in tune with her body. Maybe it was some intense level of denial; her father had died of lung cancer at the age of 63.

While playing drums while she taught, I had noticed a substantial deterioration in her dance – she moved sluggishly and tentatively. I should have known, but I attributed it to ageing. She was tickling 70 and I told myself that there was no way she could be dancing like she did 30 years ago. I should have known.

We went to Lennox Hill Hospital on Monday where my brother, Jack, a hematologist, was Chief of Medicine. Tests showed that her right lung was full of fluid. I privately asked Jack to give me three possible reasons for this fluid. He said: "1 would be cancer. 2 would be cancer. 3 would be cancer." It was the only time I held back from telling Gabrielle everything, but let that information wait two days until she, herself, heard the official diagnosis. There's always hope. The diagnosis was confirmed on Wednesday.

I should have known.

The problem, aside from cancer, was that she was scheduled to teach a weekend workshop at Omega Institute beginning that Friday and, at this point, she could barely walk. When I told her I was going to make the call to cancel the workshop, she refused. Aside from the fact that 150 people had arranged their lives to be in upstate New York, Jonny was teaching in Switzerland and would be gone for 2 weeks. She knew that if she canceled the workshop, Jonny would call to find out why (the 5Rhythms network was pervasive and instantaneous) and she did not want to give him this news over the phone, nor lie about it to him.

So, off we went on Friday for her to teach in that condition and with that knowledge. She could hardly move and, when she spoke, fluid gurgled in her throat. She told the participants that she had a mild form of pneumonia (that "lie" caused her tremendous pain as well; it was foreign to her nature to mislead that way) and that they should not expect her to do much dancing with them. But, she taught the workshop brilliantly and gave the people their money's worth.

I was the one who almost didn't make it through, but her courage and fortitude overcame the agony I experienced as I watched her struggle.

Anybody want to mess with this?

I didn't think so.

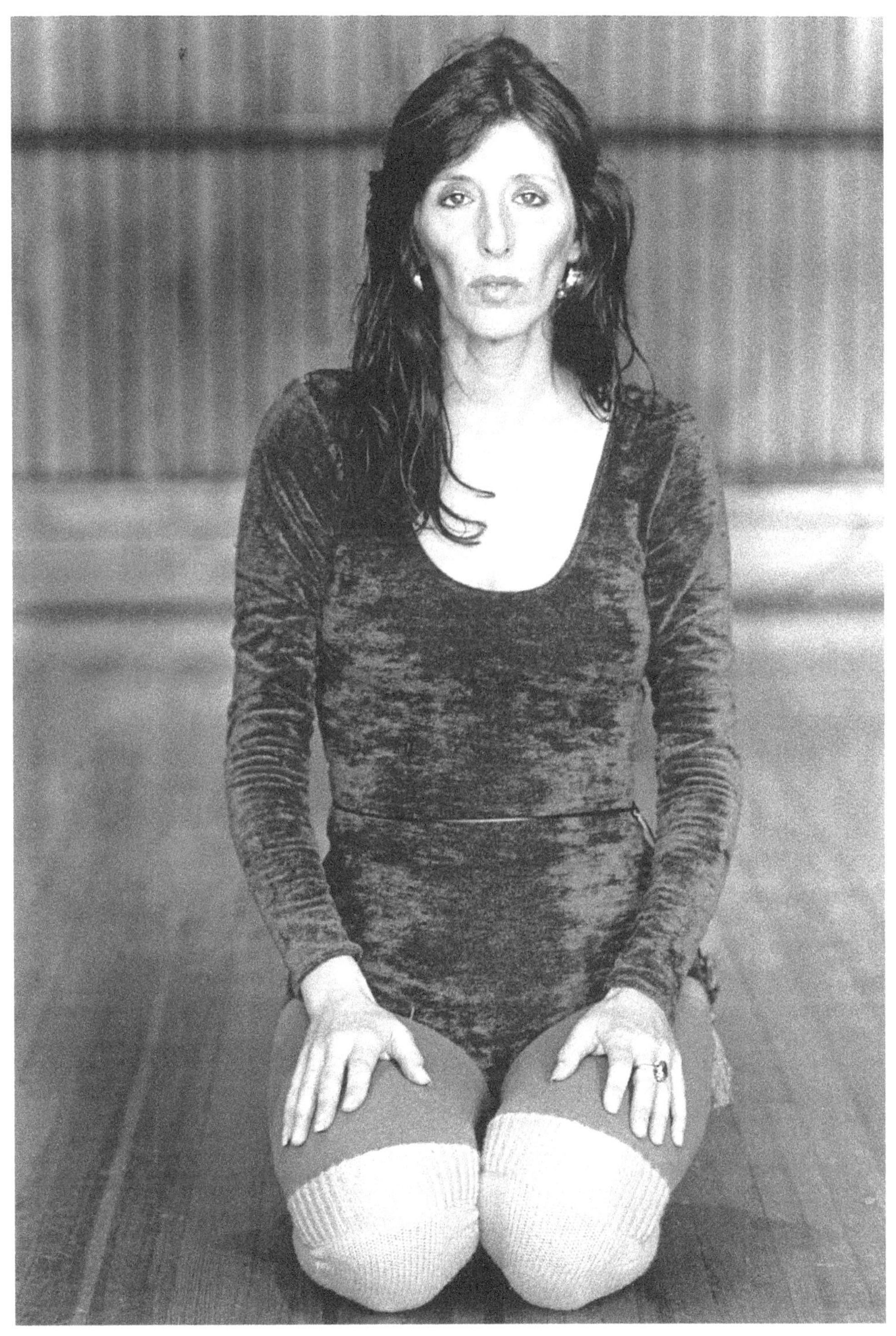

A SHOPPER

For clothes. She loved looking at clothes and she loved looking for clothes. Black clothes, mostly. And, shoes – can't forget shoes. And not necessarily for herself. One of the best things that could happen to a person was to have Gabrielle out shopping for a birthday or Christmas. She was unerring in her choices. When we went together, I would judge the quality of the stores, not by the quality of the clothes, but by the comfort of the seating while I waited.

When we first got together, she was in a purple, mauve, lilac, lavender phase (the fashion industry would wake up to this a few years later). Glorious bursts of color in everything she wore. The antique phase followed. Layers of thin material, lace, capes, scarves. It was all very sensuous and flowing and lyrical.

Gabrielle settled into black many years ago. She found her home. She was comfortable in black. Her closet was a black hole, swallowing black clothing, but occasionally letting some out. It was a nightmare for me. She would call from Germany and sweetly (very sweetly; she knew the problem) say: "Robbie, would you go into my closet so you can send me my black.............." It didn't matter what it was – sweater, shirt, pants, dancewear – I was lost. It seemed like there was a gazillion in there of each.

One of her best and dearest friends was a designer named Donna[5], a union of the ultimate shopper and the ultimate shoppee. They adored each other. Gabrielle would go to her runway shows and "seasonal" parties. Donna would come to 5Rhythms events when she could and dance her brains out. It was a marriage made in heaven, a black heaven at that. If black were a drug, Donna would be a major enabler. Many of Gabrielle's most cherished, comfortable and stylish pieces were from Donna. She was one of the very last people to see Gabrielle (bed-ridden) before she died. They threw me out of the house and had a delicious girly evening in our bedroom.

In her Last Will and Testament, Gabrielle directed that her clothing be sold at public auction (hopefully to her teachers and dancers around the globe) and that Jonny and I go on a shopping spree. We have demurred somewhat and are giving a substantial portion of the proceeds to 5RRO and Donna's foundation, Urban Zen. There will be some money left over. Who's going to shop for me?

---

[5] I'm not sure why I've adopted the convention of not using last names in this book. It seems kind of silly here, but I'm sticking with it.

Someone asked me who did the styling for this photo.

Styling? This is just the way she dressed.

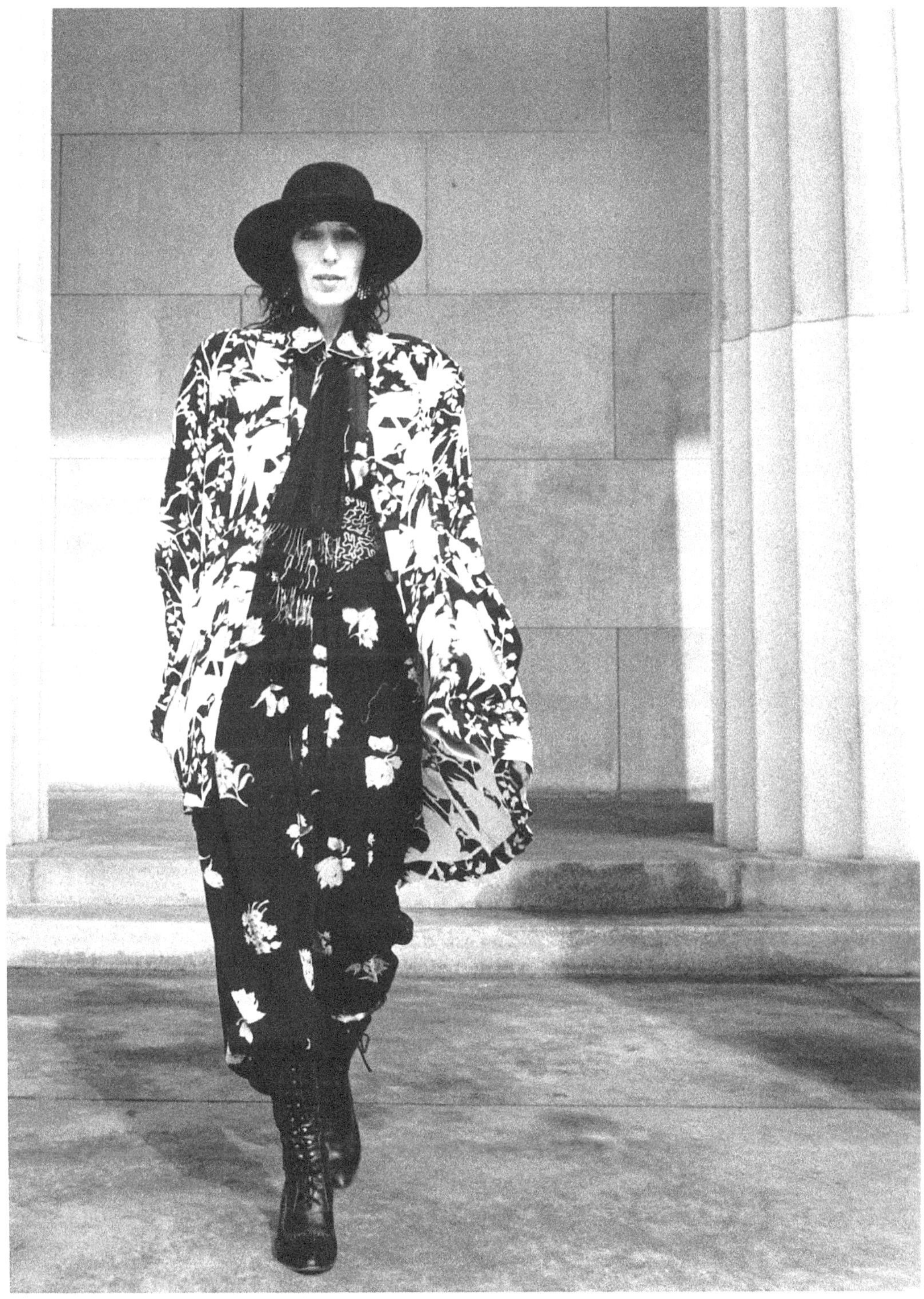

MY FOREVER

After some time in denial, I was stunned by the profound realization that I would be taking Gabrielle to her death. We never thought it would happen as it did. Most of the women in her family lived healthy, independent lives into their 90's. I was supposed to go first.

I don't have much to say about the final act of this play. It's still too painful (to me) and far too personal (for Gabrielle). She's entitled to her privacy on this. Astoundingly, some of the most joyful moments of my life happened when things were worst for her. The thrill of discovering a new body position that eased her pain. The elation at finding a tv program that would take her mind off of things for a while (especially if it had leather jackets and motorcycles). The ecstasy of coming up with a new dish to cook that she would eat and ENJOY! She never complained, never bemoaned her fate, never cursed the gods, never even became attached to the outcome of this journey. She was going to heal or she was going to die. Both outcomes were acceptable to her; she was just committed to keeping the process honest, real and endurable.

I can tell you about two events that were so typically her. On the October weekend before she died, we had scheduled (back in the Spring) a weekend workshop that was intended to be her retirement party. She kept insisting for weeks that she would be there to teach, but that became impossible when she slipped into stillness a few days before. The event drew over 150 people who arrived for the Friday night start of the workshop and the dancing was intense. Later that night, lying in bed, she came out of her stillness and raised her head from the pillow to ask: "Who are all those people dancing on the ceiling? What are they all doing there?"

On the following morning, Jonny and I alerted the world to Gabrielle's condition by email to the 5Rhythms communities around the world. We started a special Facebook page to give people a forum to express themselves and the response was overwhelming, posting after posting, comment after comment. On that Saturday evening, Gabrielle emerged from her stillness again to talk about all the people who were speaking inside her head.

She died at home, something she told me was crucial to her. Three of our sons were visiting, when, around 7:00PM, Raj, our sainted nurse, told me to take the boys out to dinner. She had the sense that the end would come soon. Nilaya stayed behind for the same reason. About ½ hour later, Nilaya texted me at the restaurant to come back immediately, and Jonny and I raced home to say good-bye.

I handled everything well except the very end. I had to leave the room when Nilaya and Lekha dressed Gabrielle (of course, Rick Owens, Donna Karan and her favorite Ann Demulemeister boots). Love and service are a powerful combination and Gabrielle was bathed in both. I contributed a beautiful white silk scarf she had given me for formal occasions. I just couldn't handle the bag and gurney. I grabbed Bertha as they wheeled her down the hallway – all I could think about was to send her off to the beat, her favorite lover (I was her second favorite lover). I was told later that the funeral home people were stunned as I drummed her out the door – out of our home, but not my heart.

I had the funny feeling she was acting out when Hurricane Sandy hit a few days after she died. I was stuck in our home – no electricity, no elevator (5th floor – it was hard for me to leave the house more than once a day), no tv, no computer, no light to read. Just me and her spirit for five days, one of the most intense experiences of my life, like she had planned some deep, final shamanic exercise or test. I kept saying to myself: "C'mon sweetheart, you're supposed to quietly exit stage left, not stage WTF is going on here."

She died in 2012— 2+1+2 = 5. She died on 10/22— 1+2+2 = 5. She died at 7:25— 7+2+5 = 14; 1+4 = 5. Somehow, I'm not surprised.

I do love this guy... We are growing old together. I see my gray hair on his head, feel my muscles tighten in his body... We've buried our fathers, put four kids through college and taken one through a marriage and divorce. We've owned two houses, said goodbye to at least four couches and three rugs. We've met each other's childhood friends and cruised the neighborhoods where we grew up. We've met a few of each other's ex-lovers and lived through it. And we've made a lot of music together.

He breaks in my jeans, gives me the olive from his martini, sends me flowers for no reason, edits my writing, massages the dreams trapped in my thighs and has more faith in me than I can muster for myself. I married a kind, loving man like my dad.

...He is part of me. I can't imagine any other. Isn't love strange?

About three months after she left, Jonny and I hosted the Memorial for her in an ornate ballroom in lower Manhattan. Over 350 people showed up to honor her. I had to explain to them that we would not spend the evening talking about Gabrielle. She and I had discussed the possibility, then the probability, then the inevitability of this event on several occasions and she pleaded with me not to allow it to become a group of people standing around talking about her. "I couldn't bear that," she said. I told her I didn't understand the problem since she wasn't going to be there. "Oh yes, I will," she replied. "Play drums and let the people dance!" So, Sanga and I played drums. The people danced. They danced their sorrow, they danced the pain of this loss, and they danced in joyful tribute to the funky elegance of her indomitable spirit.

I guess it's pretty obvious that I absolutely adored this lady, why I adored this lady, for how long I adored this lady and how blessed I was to have this lady to adore. She turned me on and filled me up.

She was my Muse.

She was my hero.

She still is.

So, goodbye my dearest one. You were, as our friend Tom from Germany once remarked, the most human being ever!

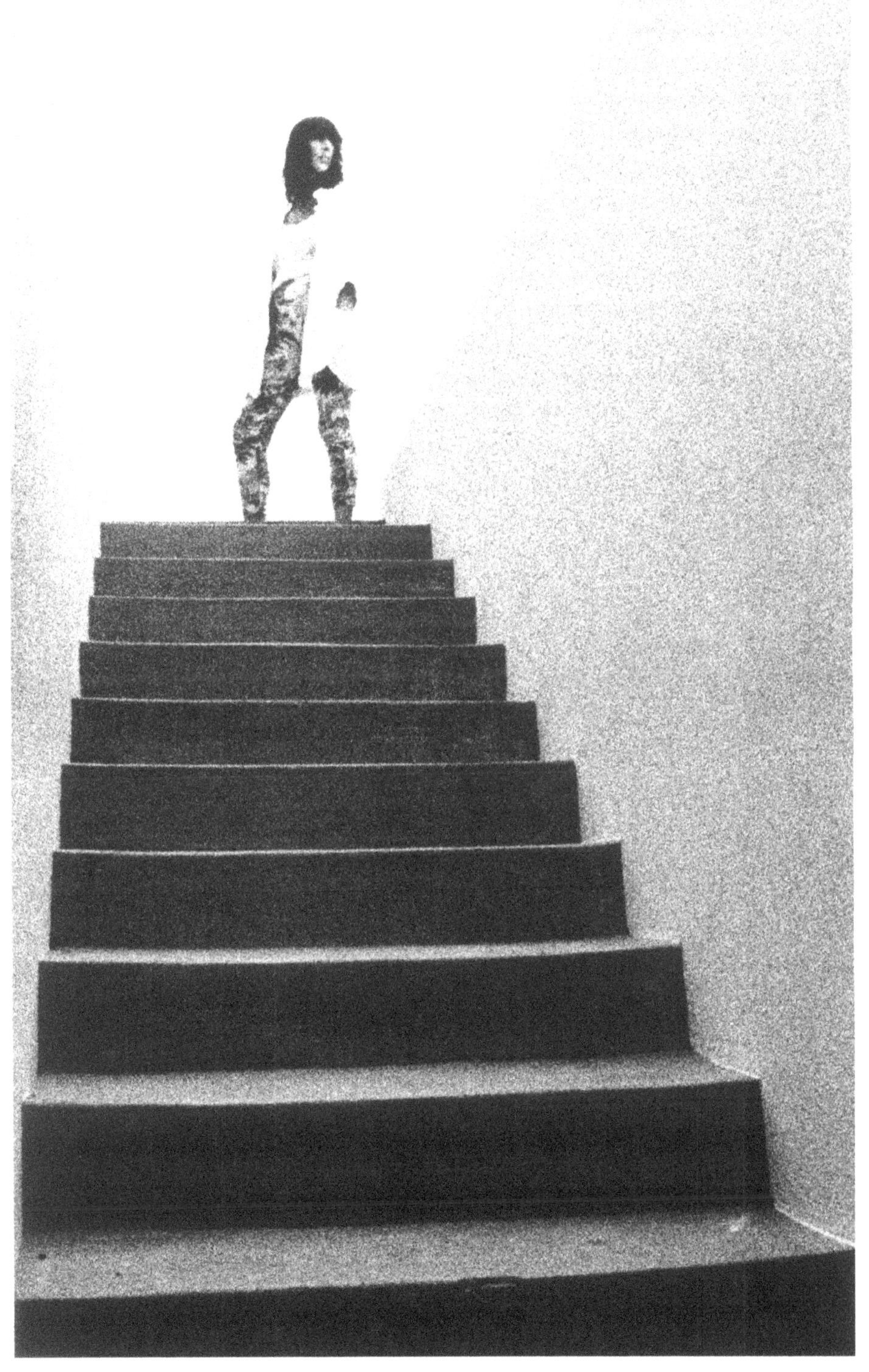

Nilaya took this photo about 2 weeks before Gabrielle died.
We were sitting on the couch in our living room.

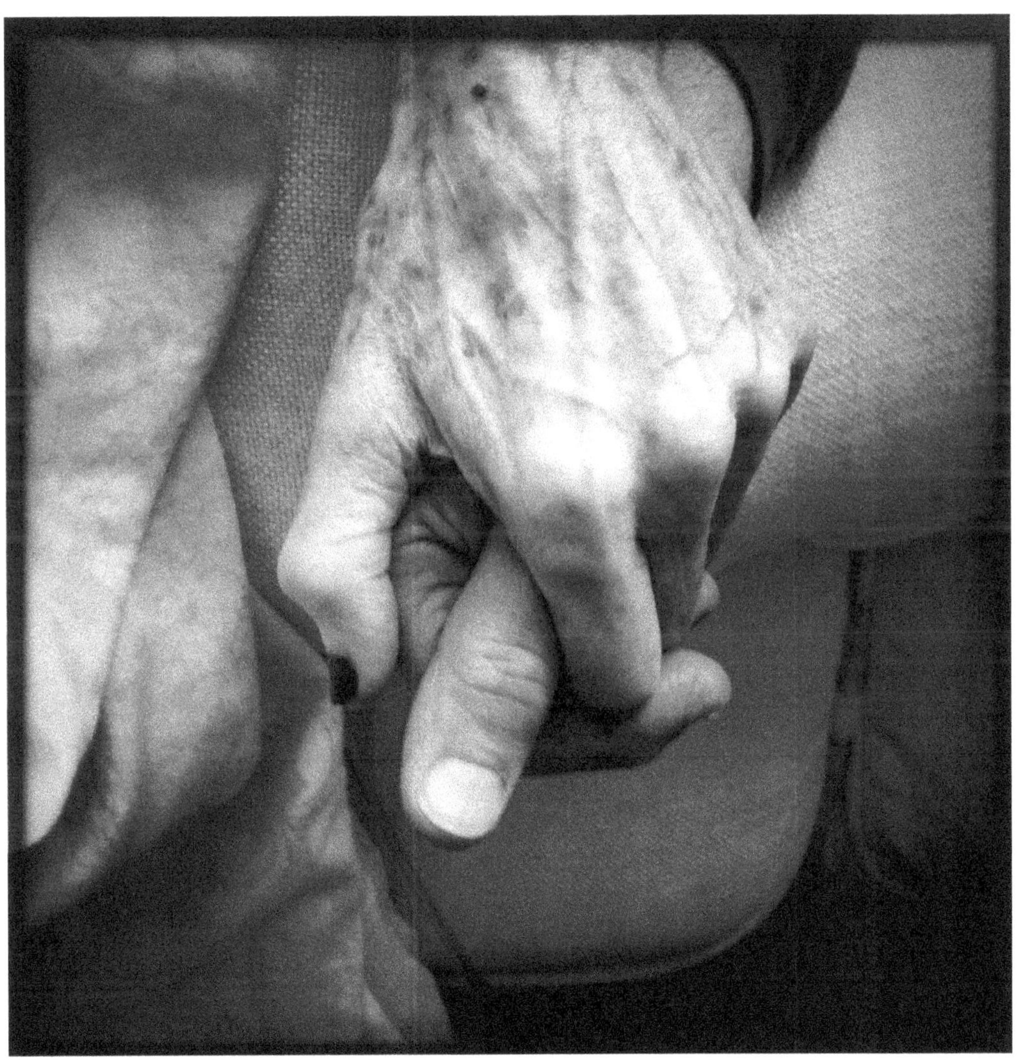

THE GIFT OF GAB

GABRIELLE SAID...

(AMONG OTHER THINGS)

Rhythm is our mother tongue.

The fastest way to still the mind is to move the body.

Put the psyche in motion and it will heal itself.

There is no dogma in the dance.

My body is a begging bowl for spirit.

After you jump and before you land, is god.

If you want to be fascinating, be fascinated.

There's only one of us here and it might not be the one you think.

Sweat your prayers.

Do you have the discipline to be a free spirit?

The body is the spirit's wife.

The body doesn't lie.

All bodies are equal – ask any earthquake.

It is not about getting lost in the dance, but being found in the dance.

The beat is a lover that never disappoints and, like all great lovers, it demands 100% surrender.

You are not in your body; your body is in you.

When I surrender to the dance, I am most vulnerable and, therefore, most powerful.

Once you get out of the way, the way becomes you and you become the way.

Between the head and feet of every person is a billion miles of unexplored territory.

The body is a Cathedral of Bones.

Energy moves in waves. Waves move in rhythms. Rhythms move in patterns. Patterns move in cycles. A human being is just that – energy, waves, rhythms, patterns and cycles. Nothing more. Nothing less. A dance.

I spoke to god one day and I asked if there was any message for the people back here and god said: "Yes. Tell them to flirt."

Why bother to take ecstasy when you can become it?

If you don't do your dance, who will?

All this dance is bullshit if we don't take it out into the street.

Saving it for later?

Put your mind in your feet and your body in the beat.

I'm not interested in enlightenment. I want to be delighted, not enlightened.

If you want to dance like me, then dance like you.

As soon as you compare yourself, you lose.

Don't be afraid to shine your light. If it ends up being too much for people, tell them to wear sunglasses!

To sweat is to pray, to make an offering of your innermost self. Sweat is holy water, prayer beads, pearls of liquid that release your past.

I love you, Robbie.

There's no such thing as maybe. If it's not yes, it's no.

When in doubt, do nothing.

If you're not living on the edge, you're taking up too much space.

Do you really think this practice is about dancing?

Life is the master; teachers come and go.

A strong romantic relationship will have a healthy balance of masculine and feminine energies, no matter what kind of bodies they come in.

You have to be home for someone to visit.

The tragedy of being self-conscious is that nobody is looking.

In life we have the opportunity to lead or follow; mostly we just resist.

It's not about being a teacher, but being a teaching.

Dance is the fastest, most direct route to the truth—not some big truth that belongs to everybody, but the get down and personal kind, the what's-happening-in-me-right-now kind of truth.

Mine is the art of inspiring people to turn themselves inside out, transform their suffering into art, their art into awareness, and their awareness into action.

Movement is my medicine, my meditation, my metaphor, and my method.

What will I find on the other side of all that I know?

I believe in the power of motion, the wisdom of gravity, the emptiness of true love, the fact that there is no way out but through the body, no way up unless we all go together, no way down unless we follow the beat, no way in unless we embrace the dark.

Many of my favorite shamans are rock stars. They probably don't even know they're shamans, but they know how to get to ecstasy and back and how to take others with them. They may not have a license, but they know how to drive.

Shed the past, forget the future and fall into the moment feet first.

God is the dance and the dance is the way to freedom and freedom is our holy work.

If you're not in your own flow, you're in somebody else's way.

There are only two positions worthy of our attention: knowing we are everything and knowing we are nothing. When we insist on being or not being something, that's when the trouble starts.

You can't see anybody when you are busy judging yourself.

The beat is a great lover – it carried me into this egoless, timeless state of being – nothing was happening, but it was electric. There was no drug, there was nothing that could compete with it, and of course all I wanted to do was take everybody else there. Who wouldn't want that experience? But you can't get it in a pill, it comes in surrender. And in order to surrender we have to be willing to let go of everything that's in the way, let go of our stress and our boredom, let go of our thinking, let go of our judgments and criticism, we have to let go of all the emotional baggage we're carrying, fear from 10 years ago, anger from 20 years ago. We have to be able to give it all up in order to go to that incredible ecstatic place. And once there, it's like god's drug. You just want it. You want to go back – you can't help it – you want to go back. It's like being a surfer, because you never know in the dance when you're going to get there, but you show up and you move, and someday the big wave comes and it just carries you.

THE GRACE OF ROTH

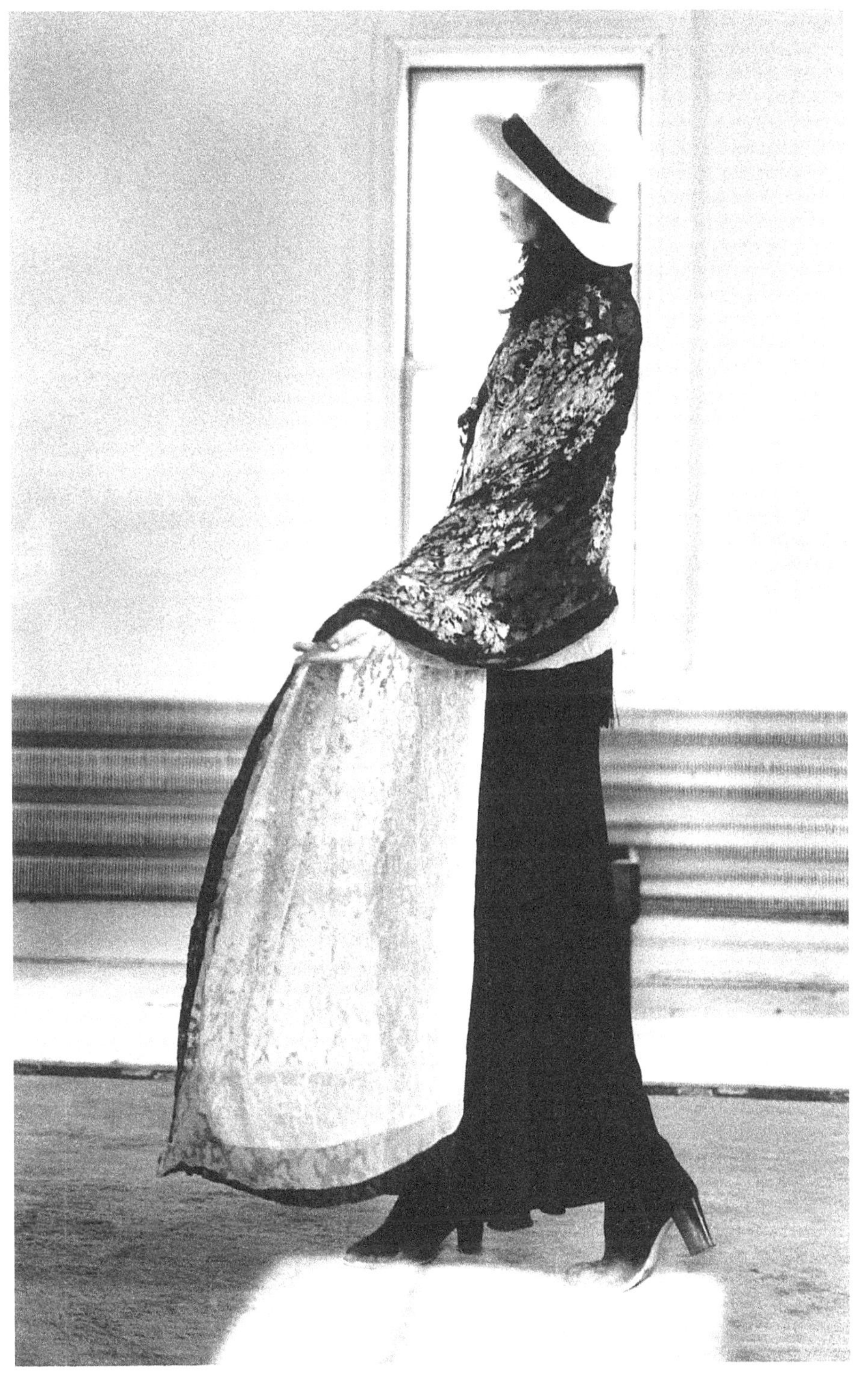

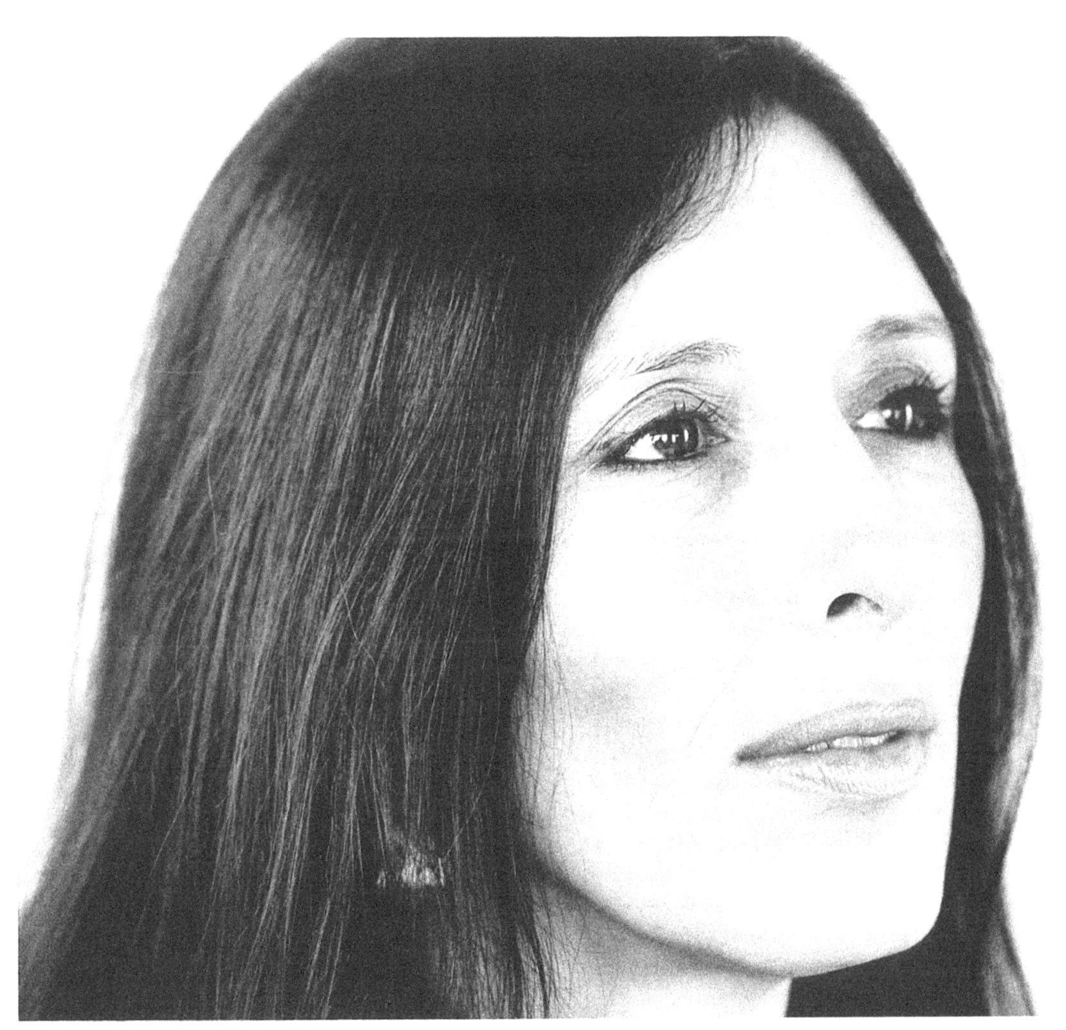

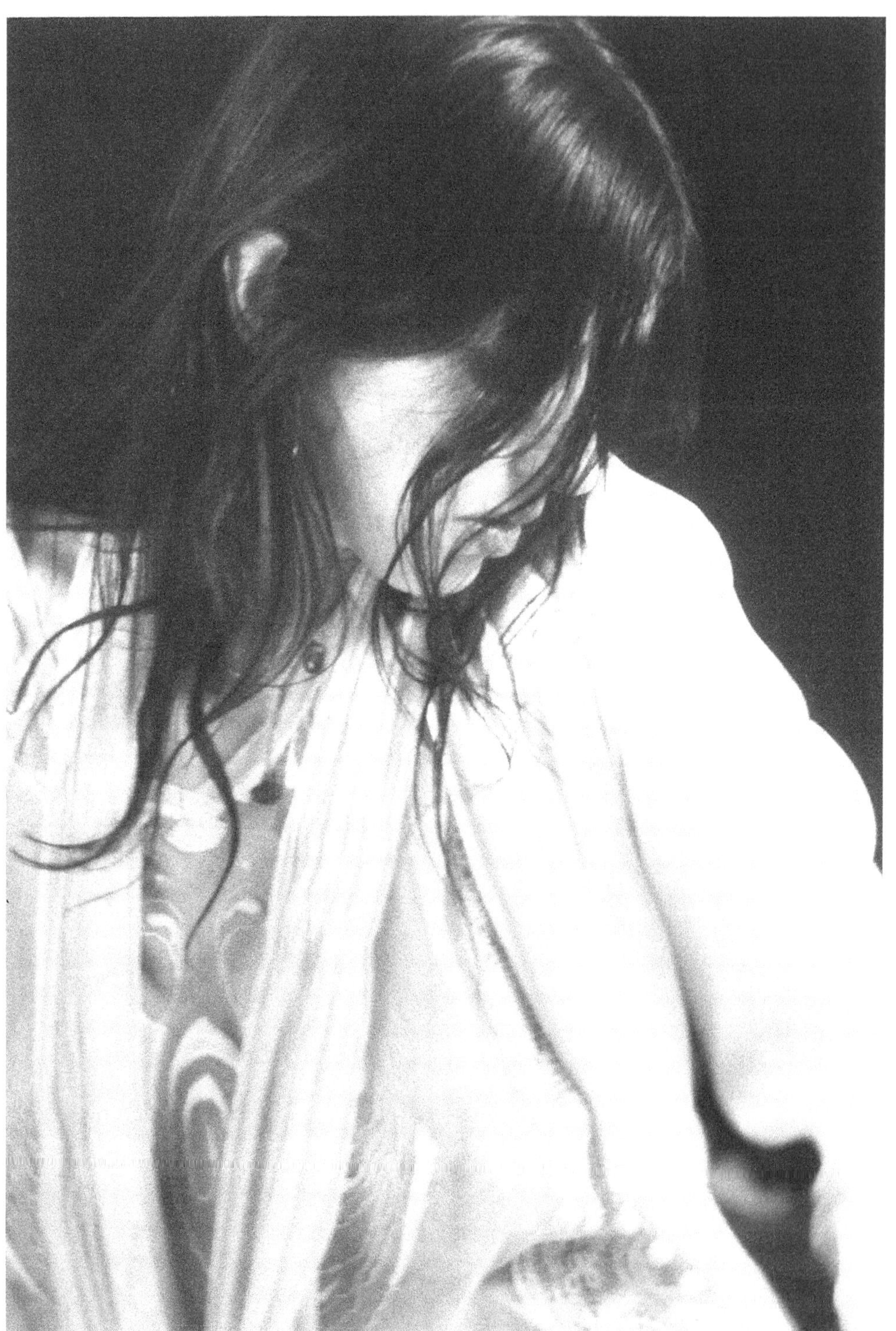

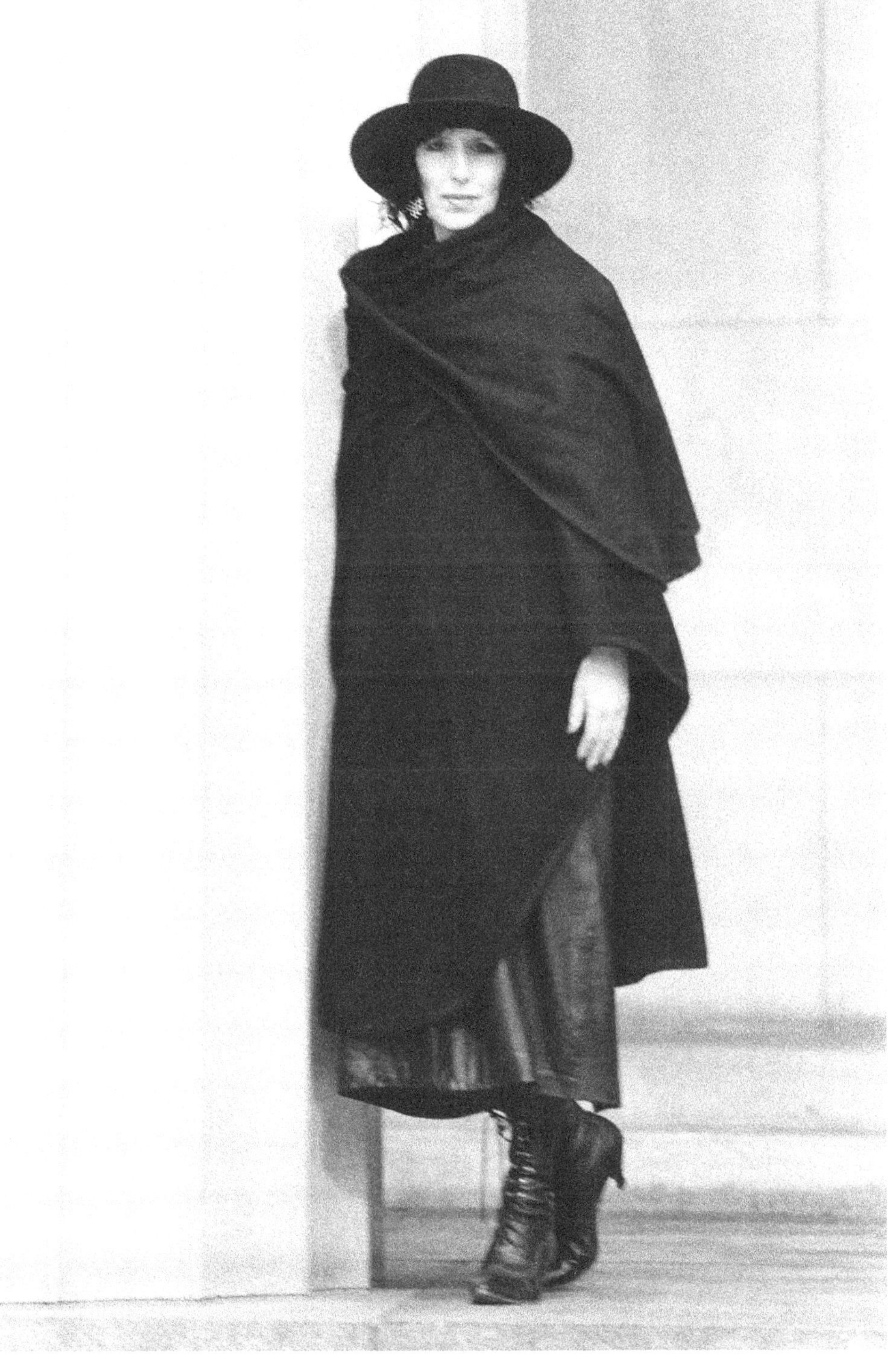

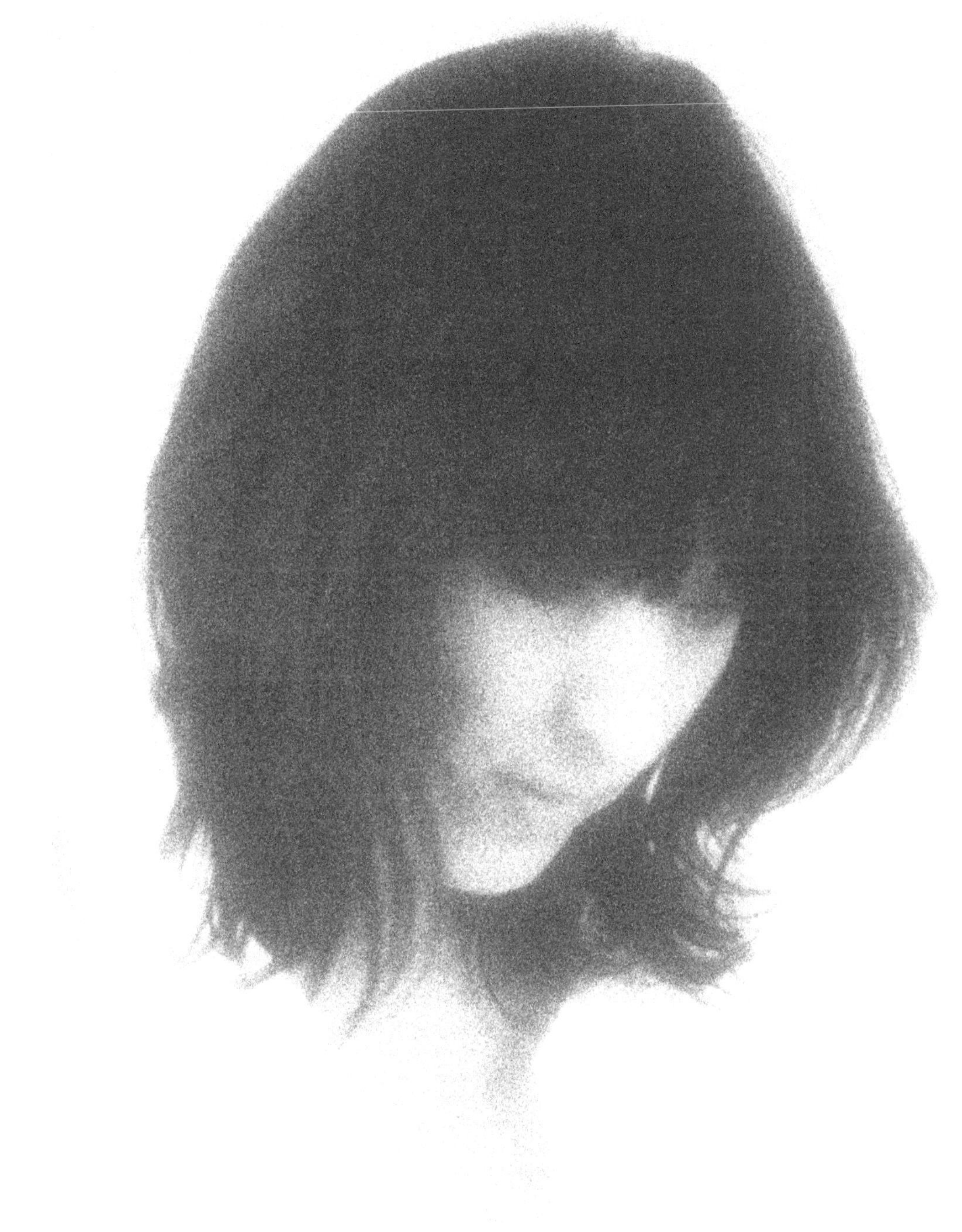

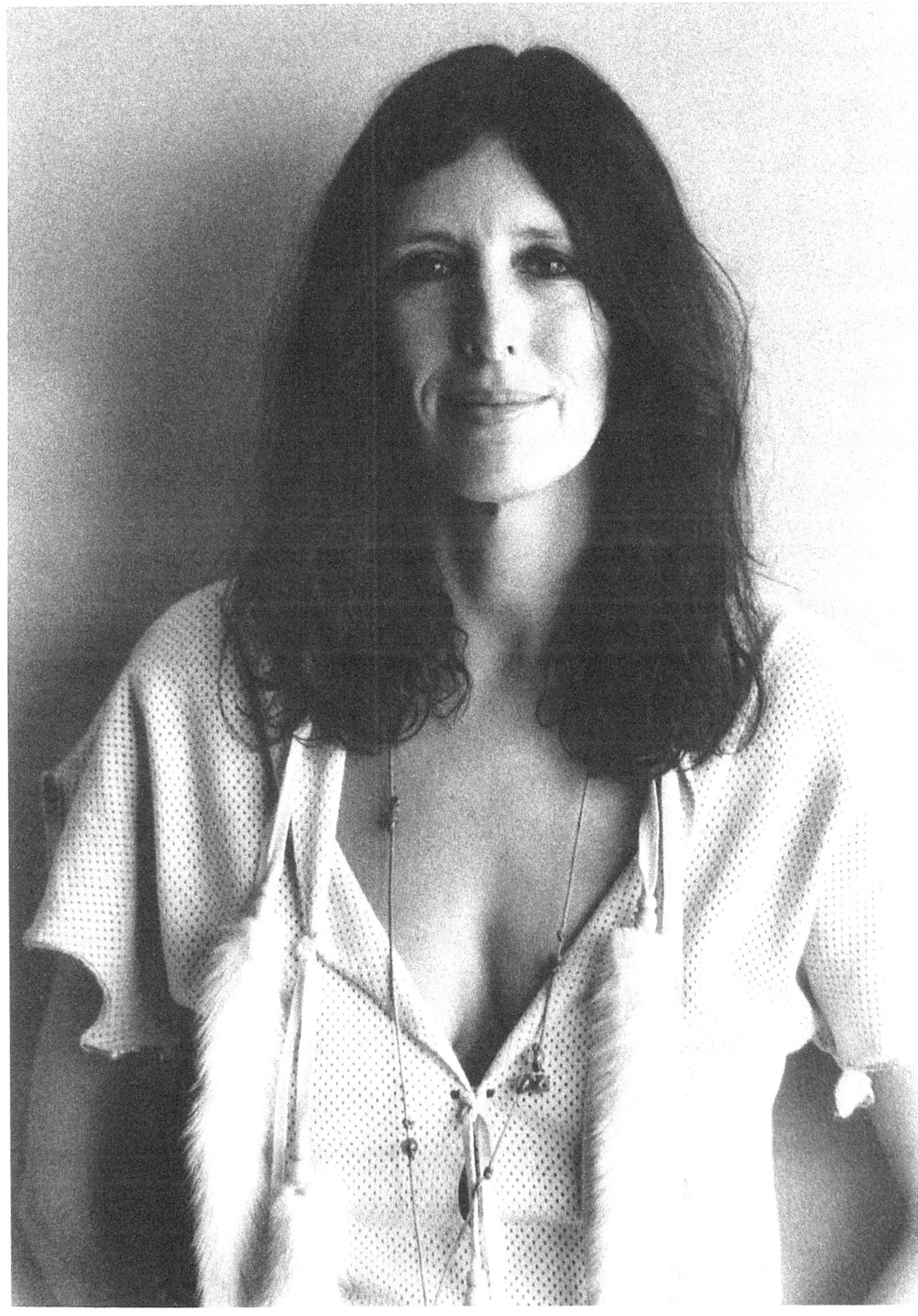

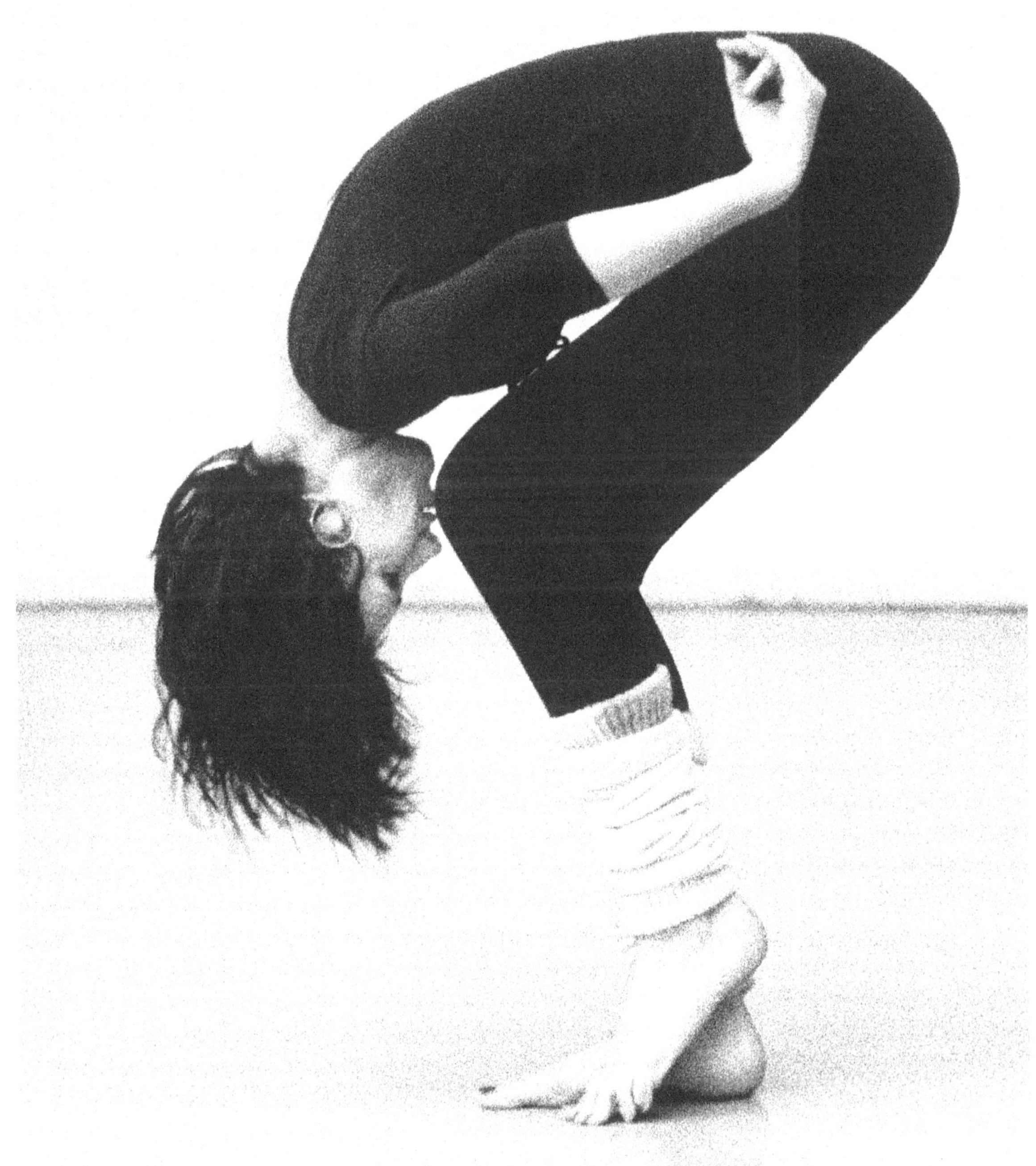

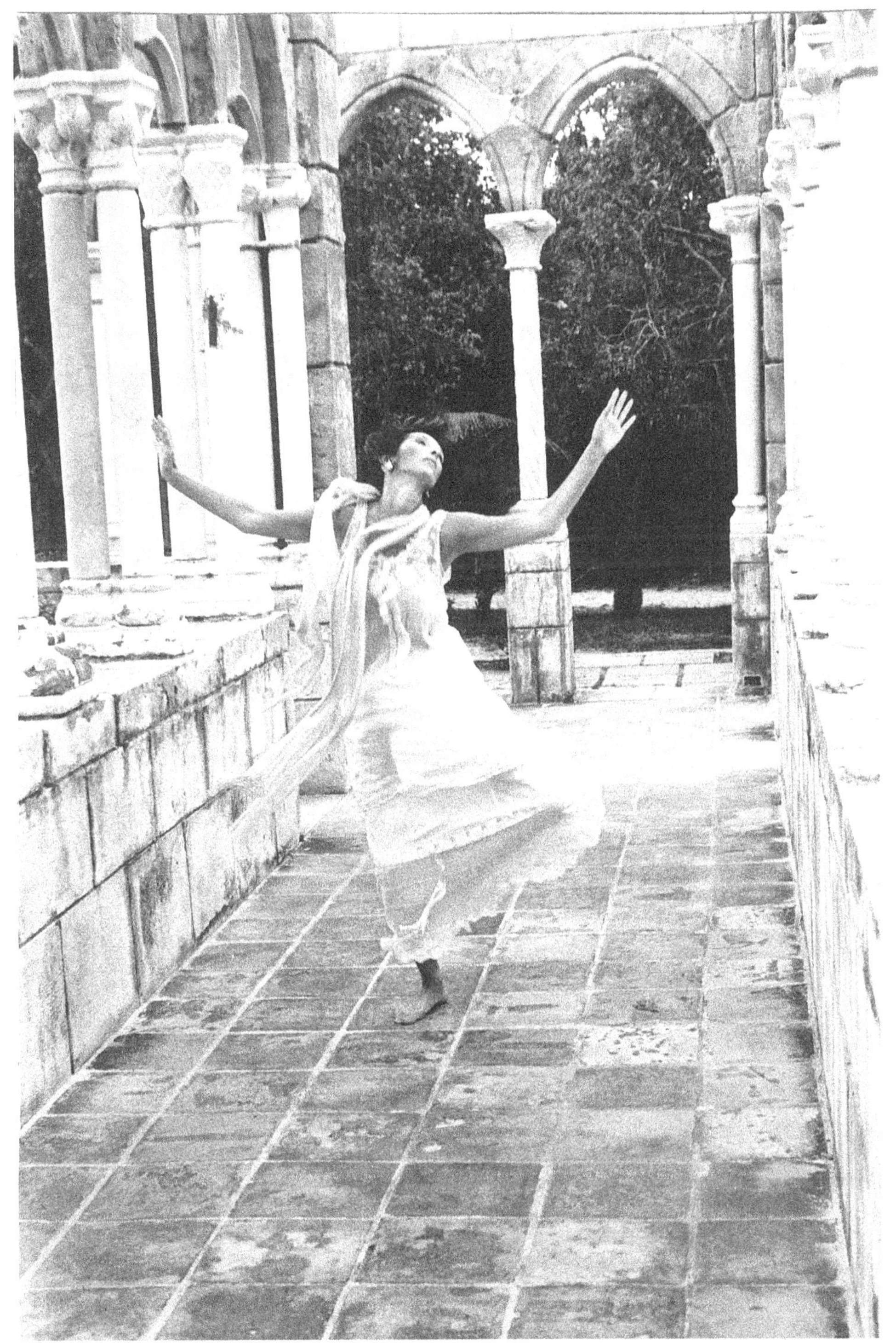

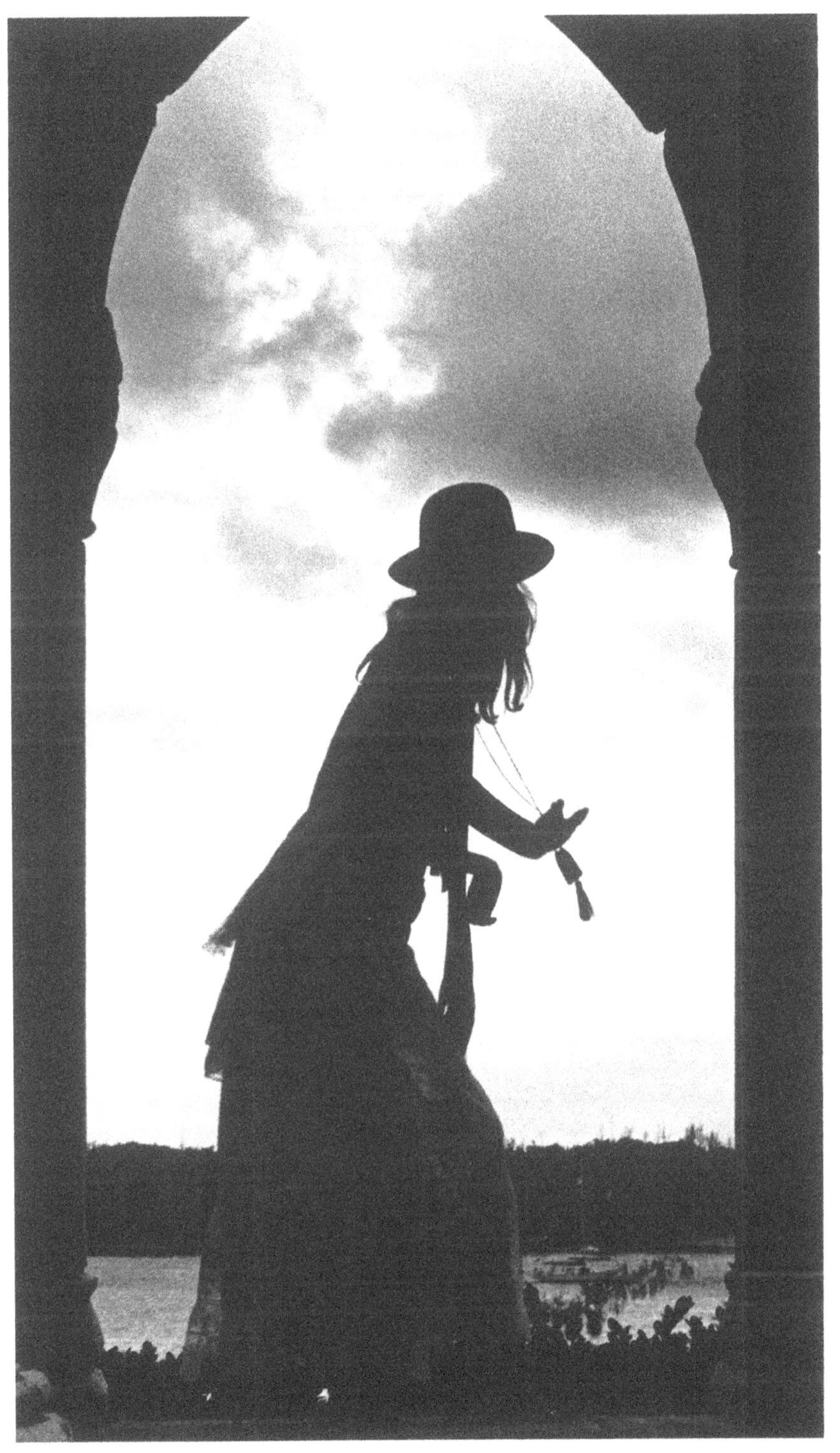

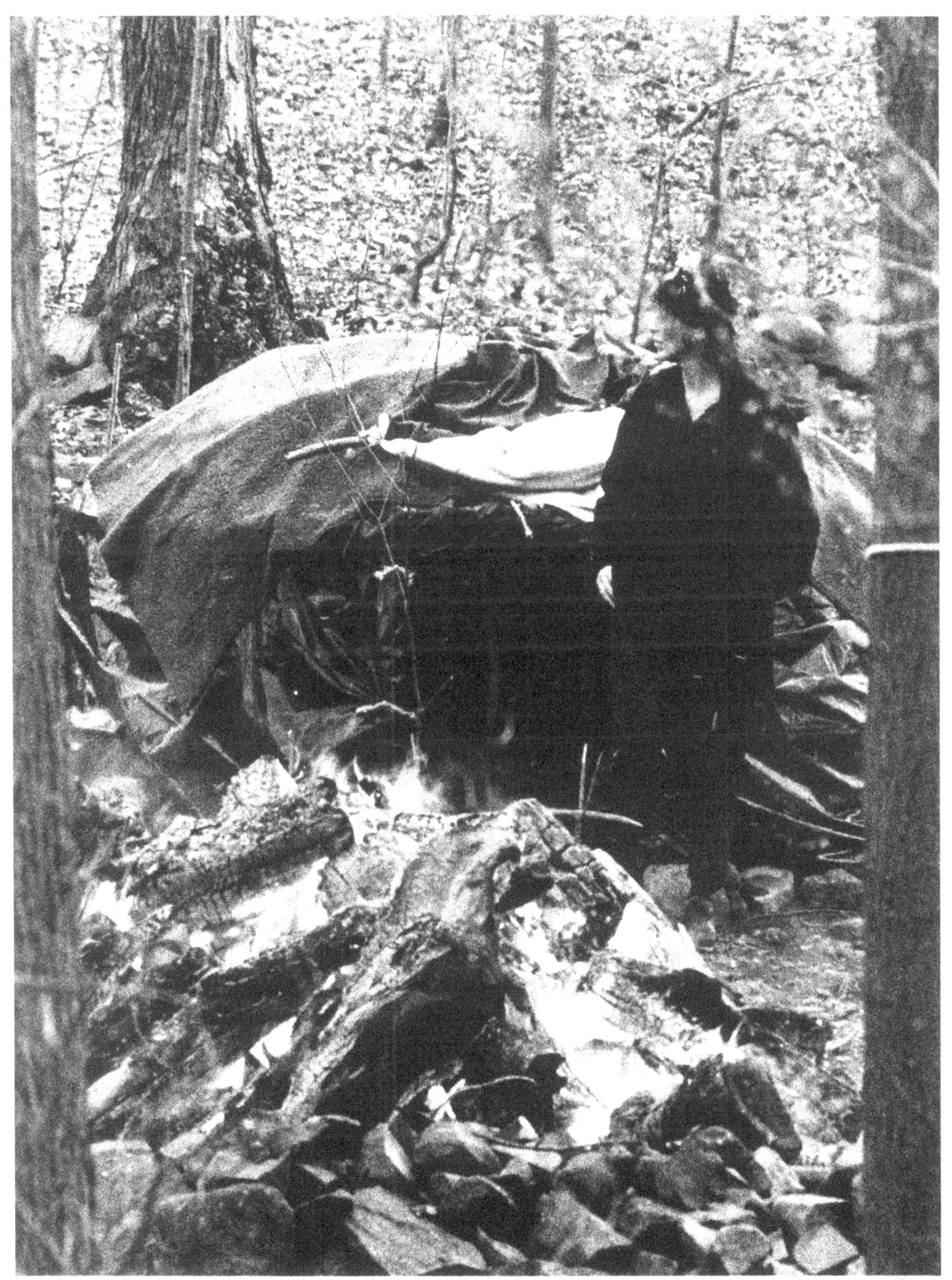

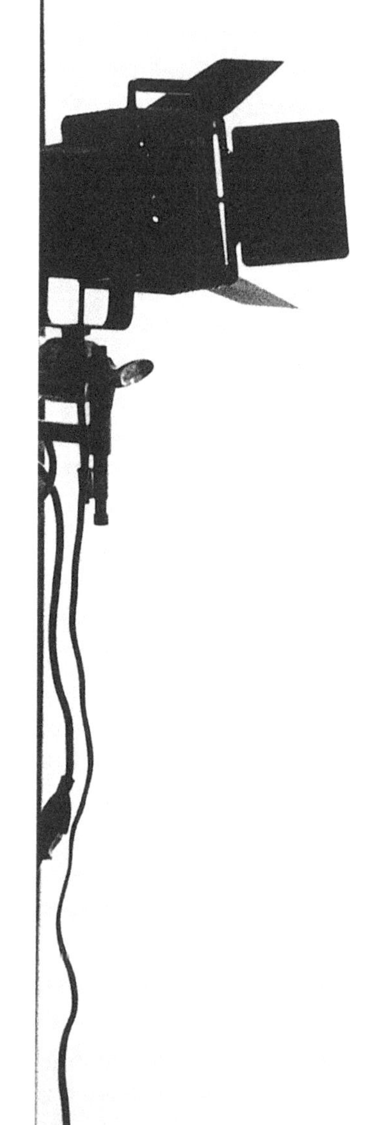

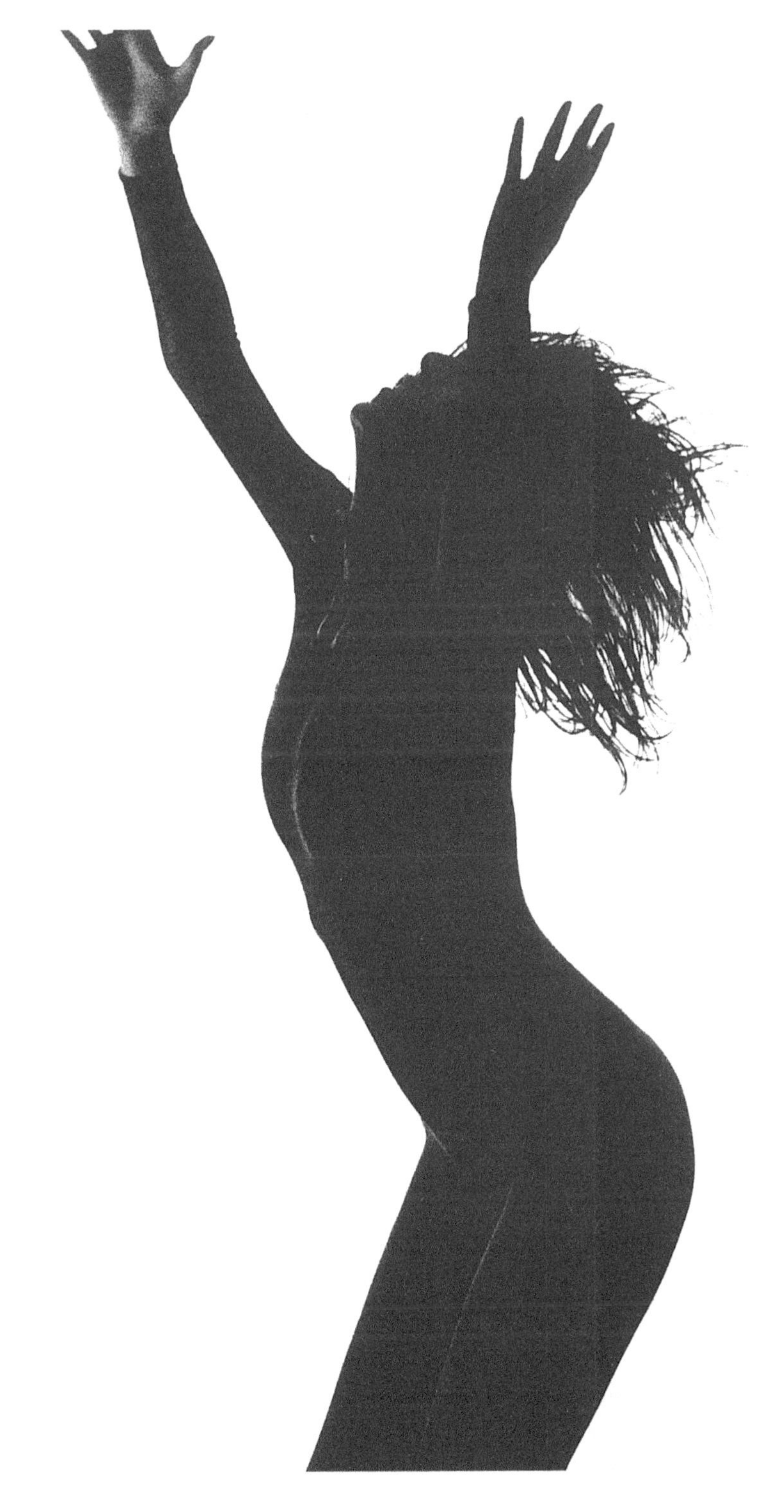

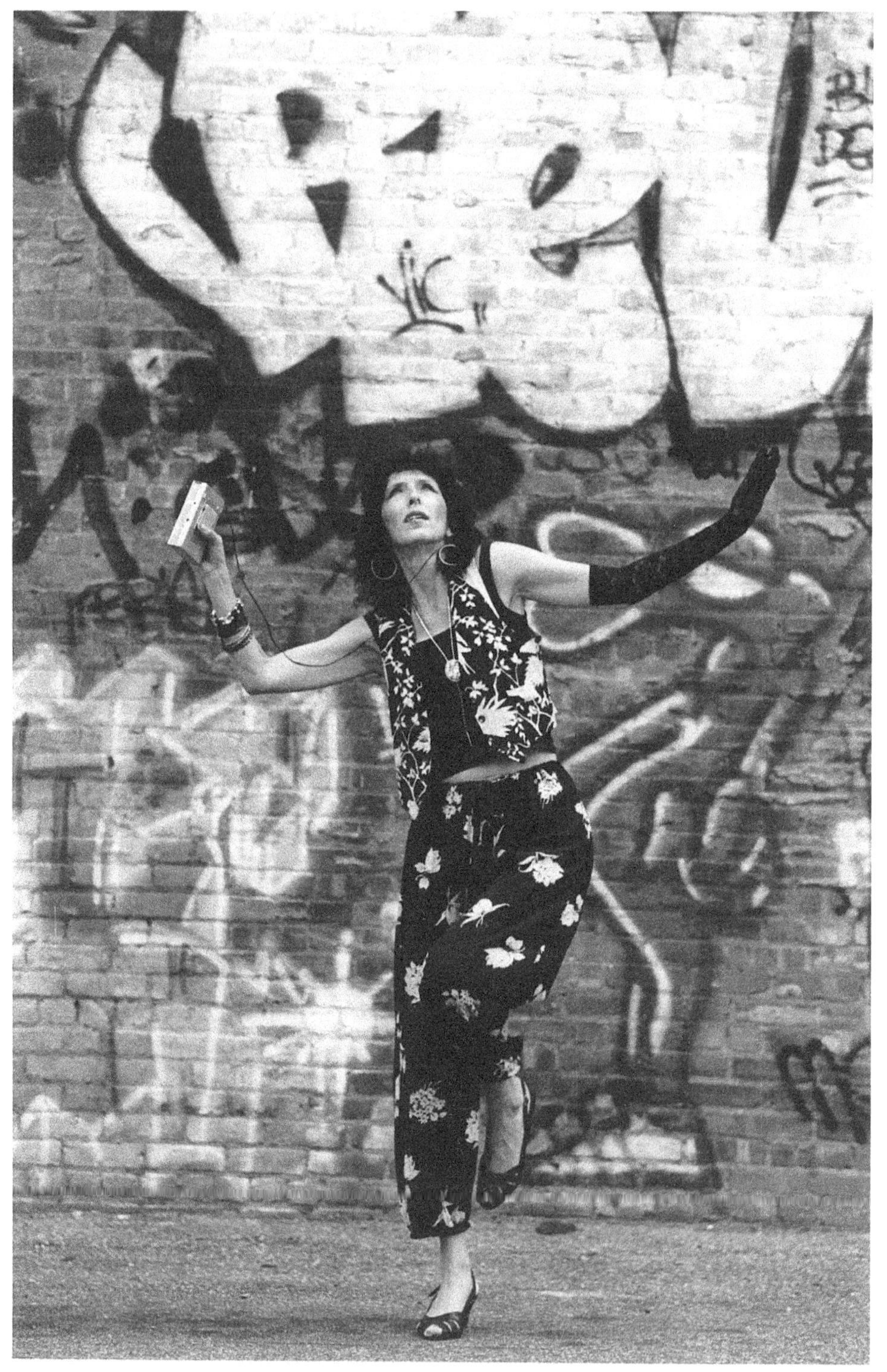

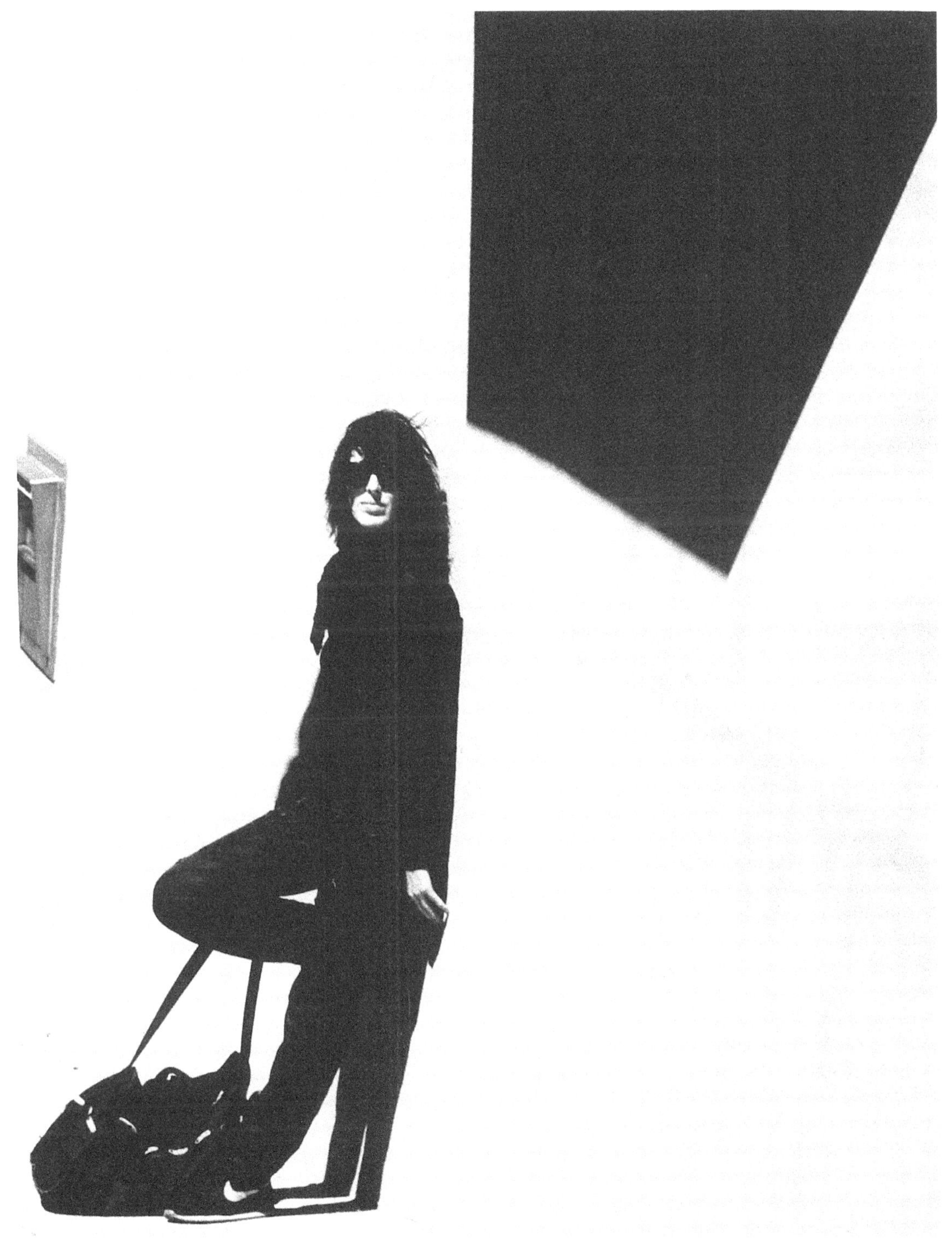

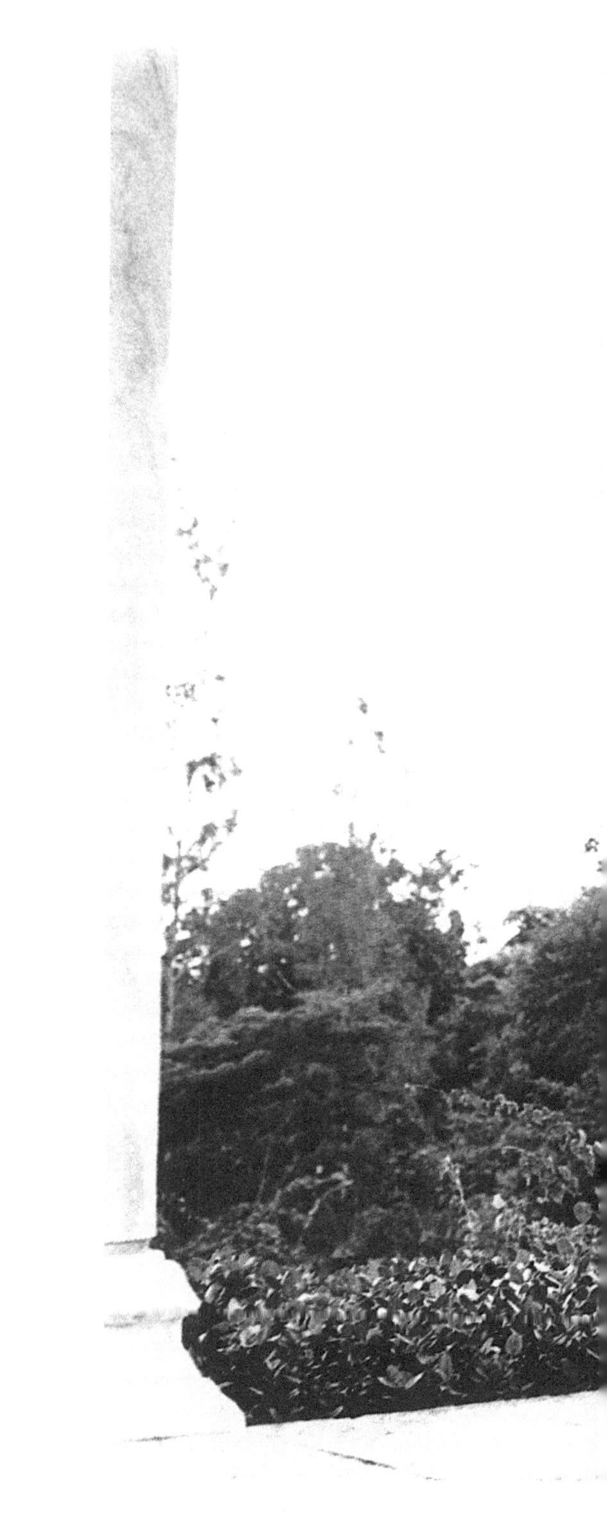

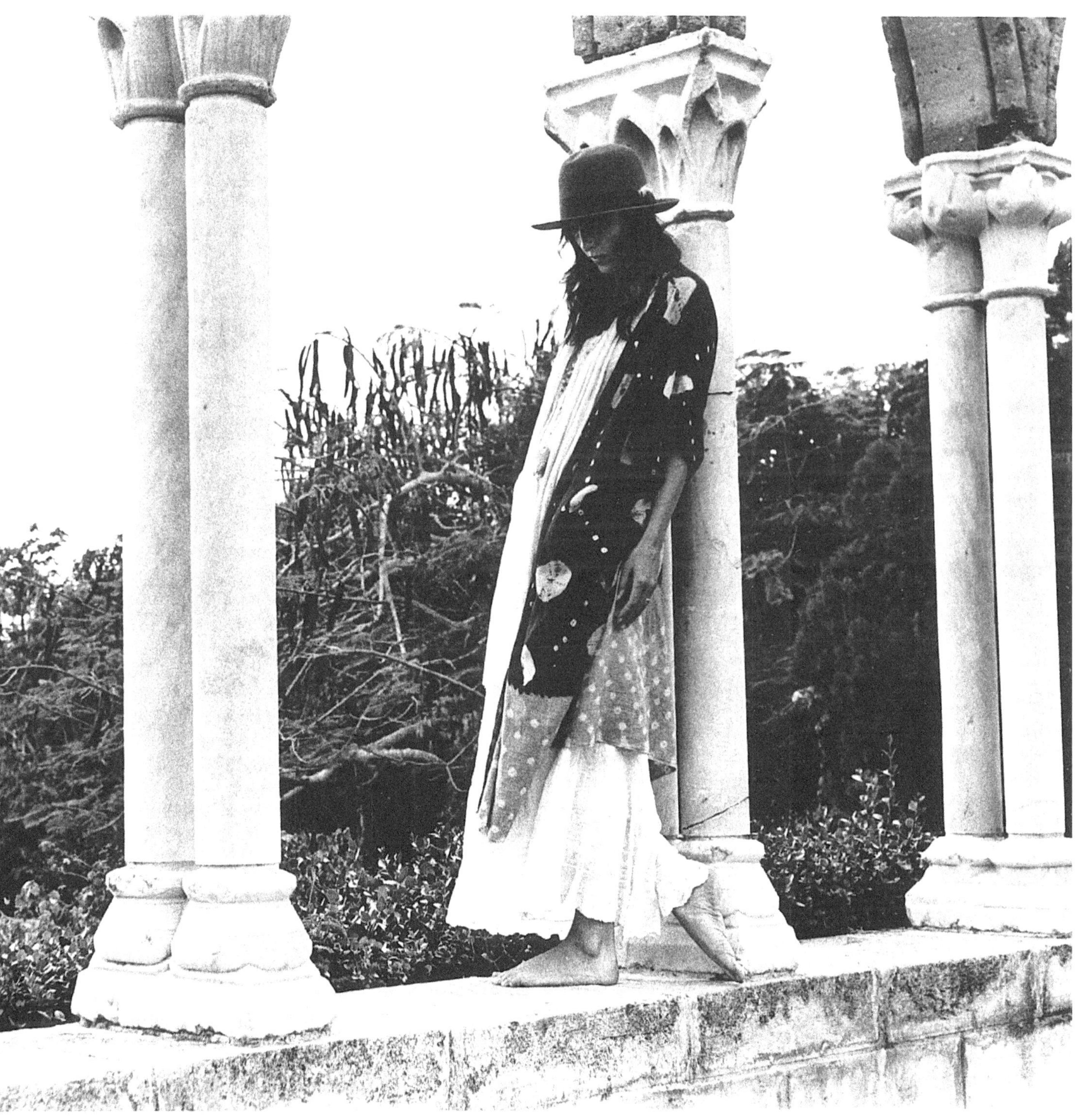

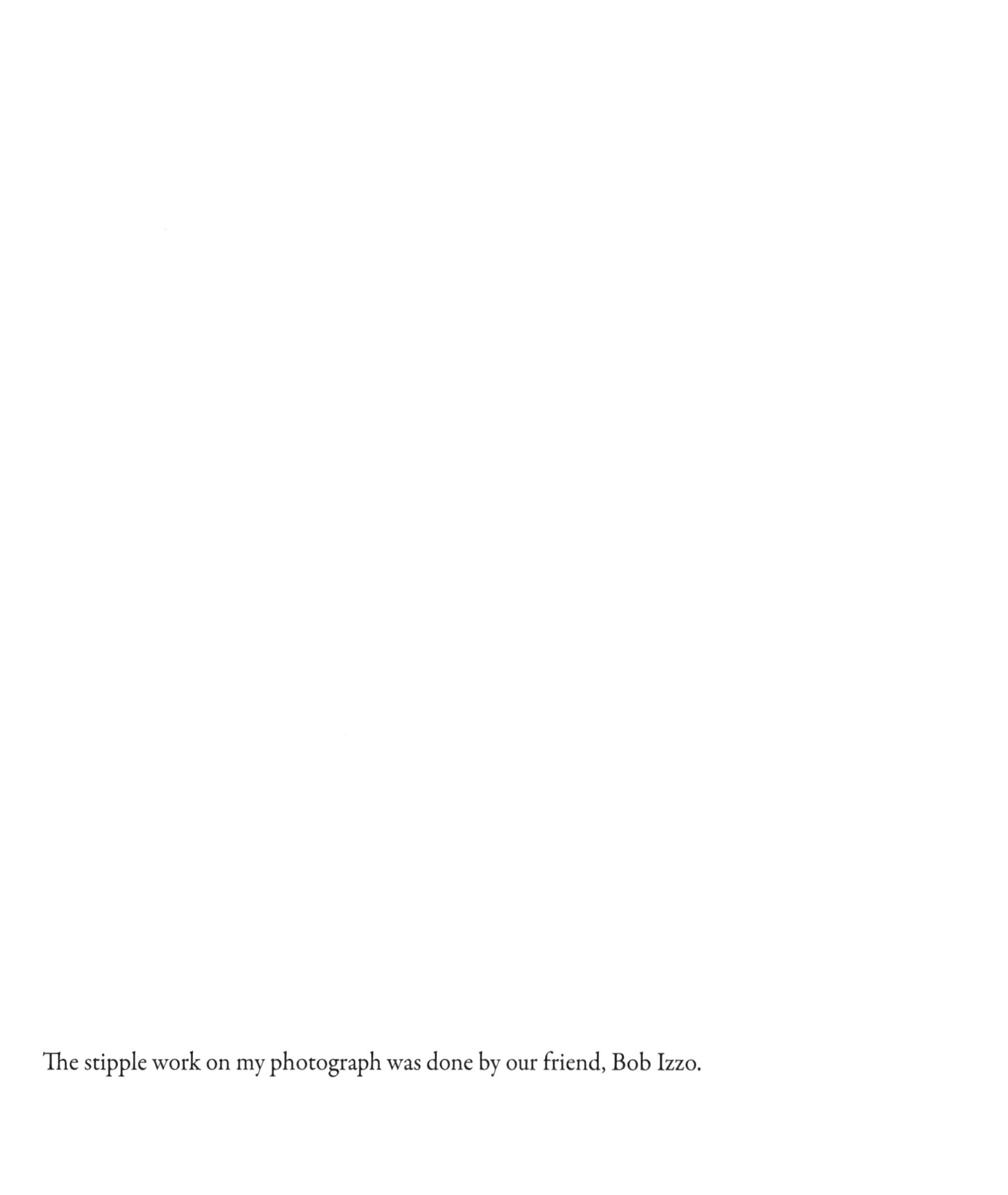

The stipple work on my photograph was done by our friend, Bob Izzo.

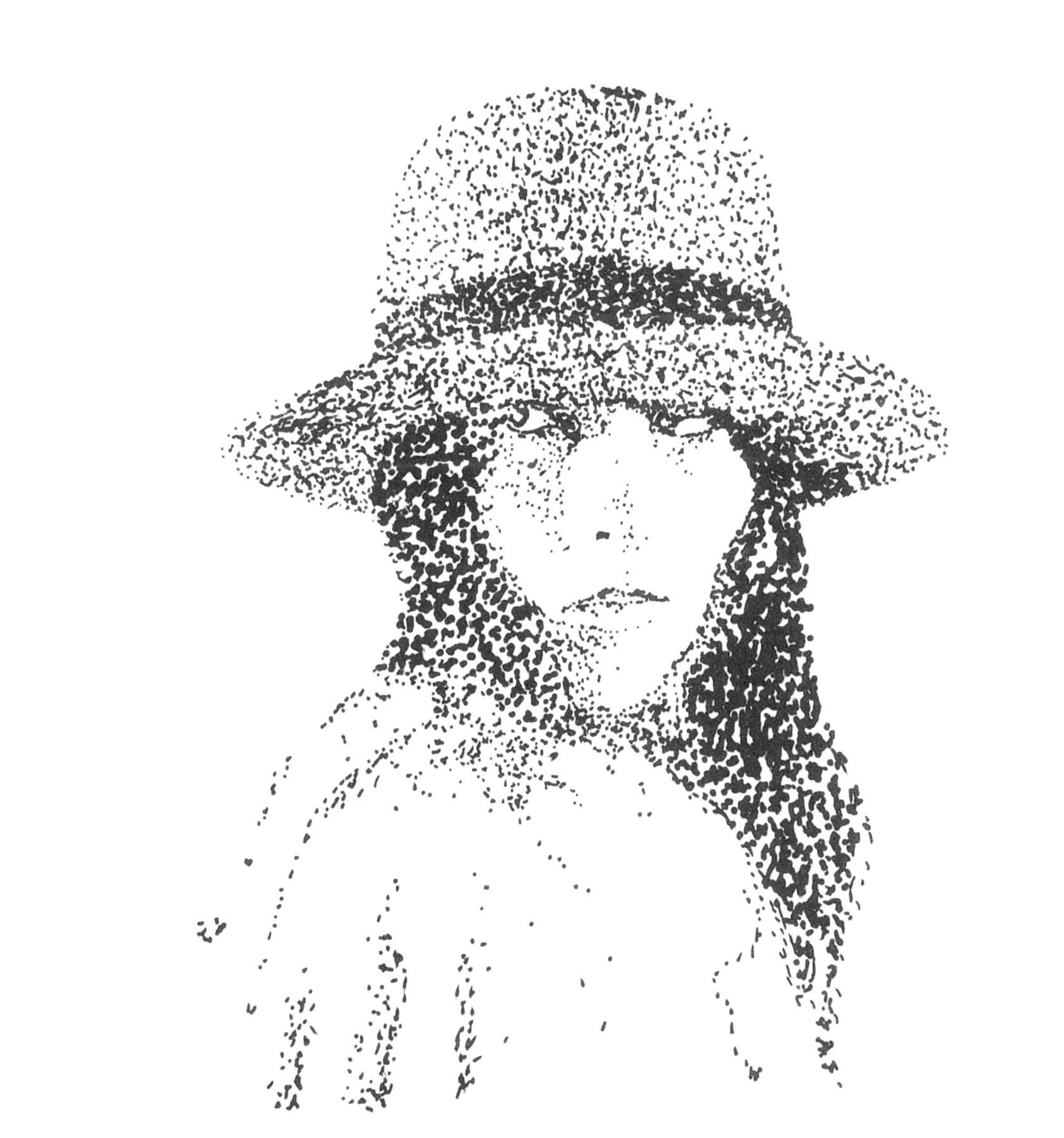

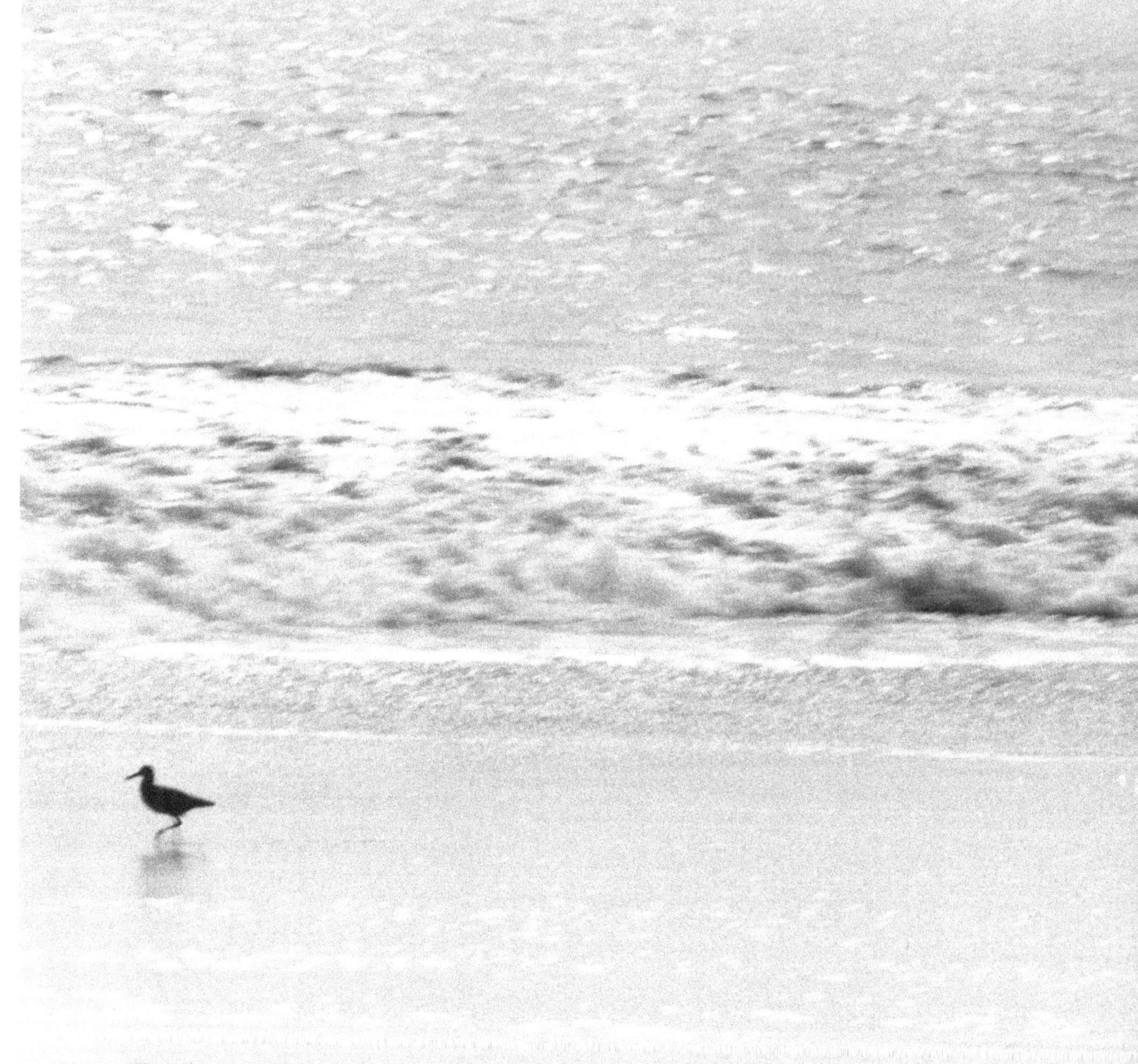

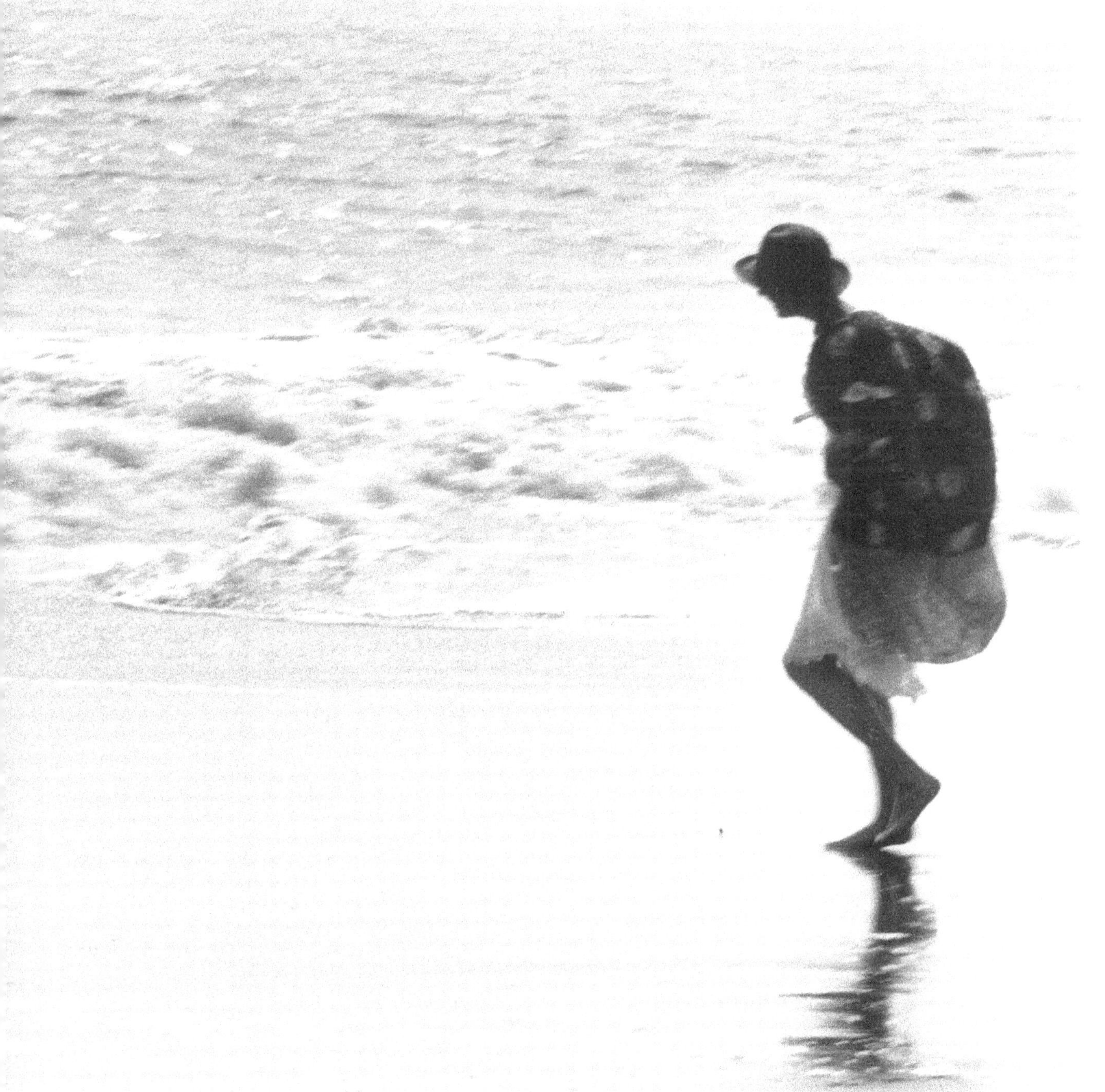

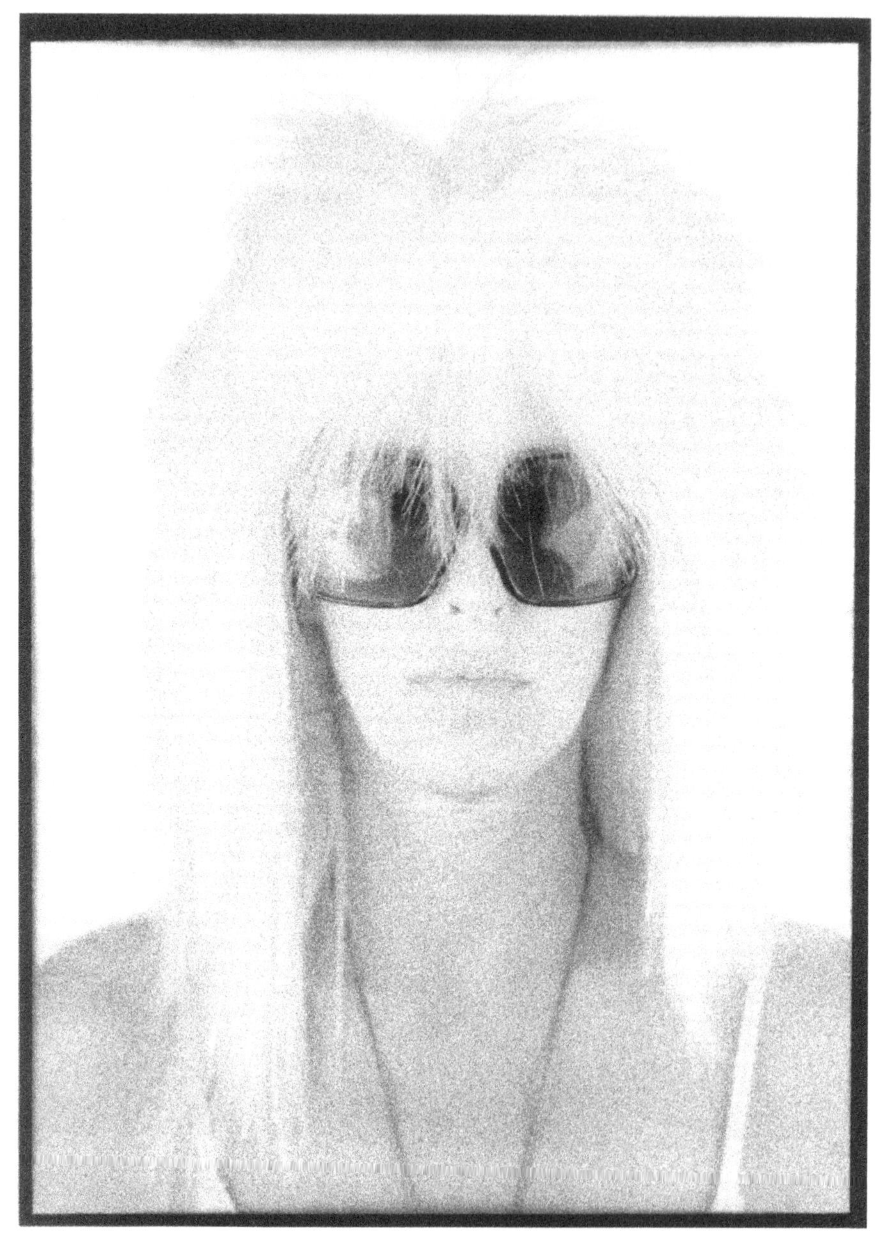

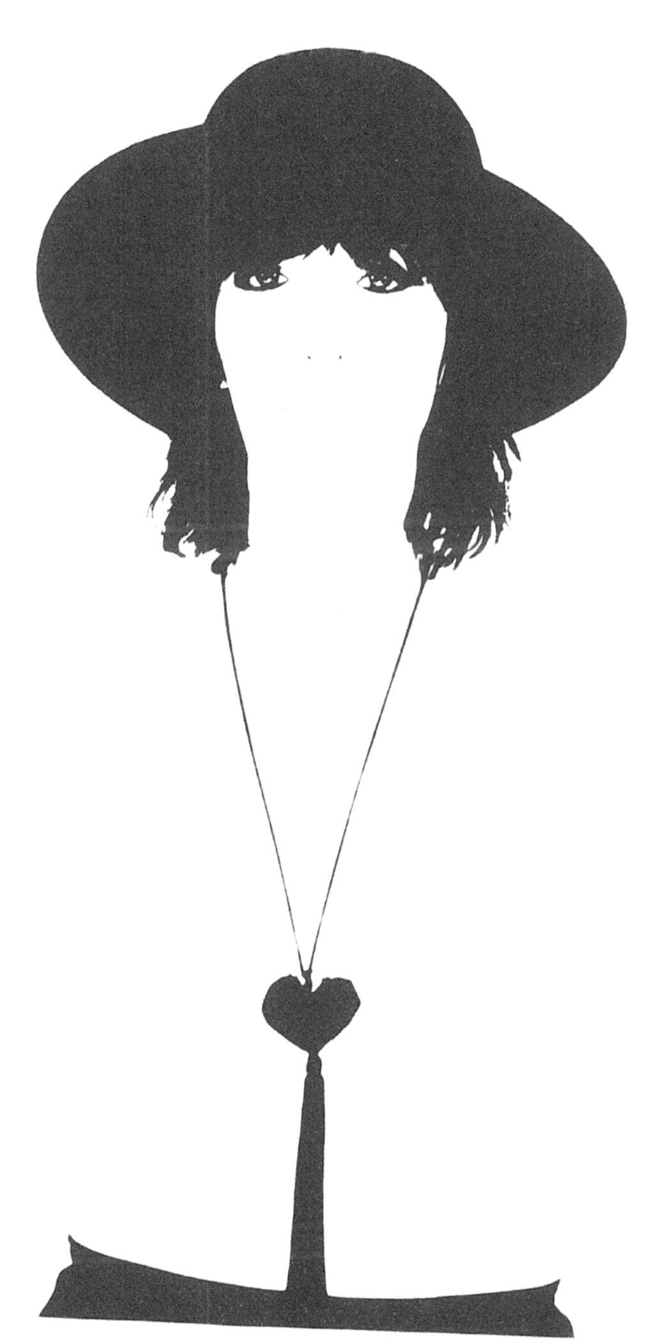

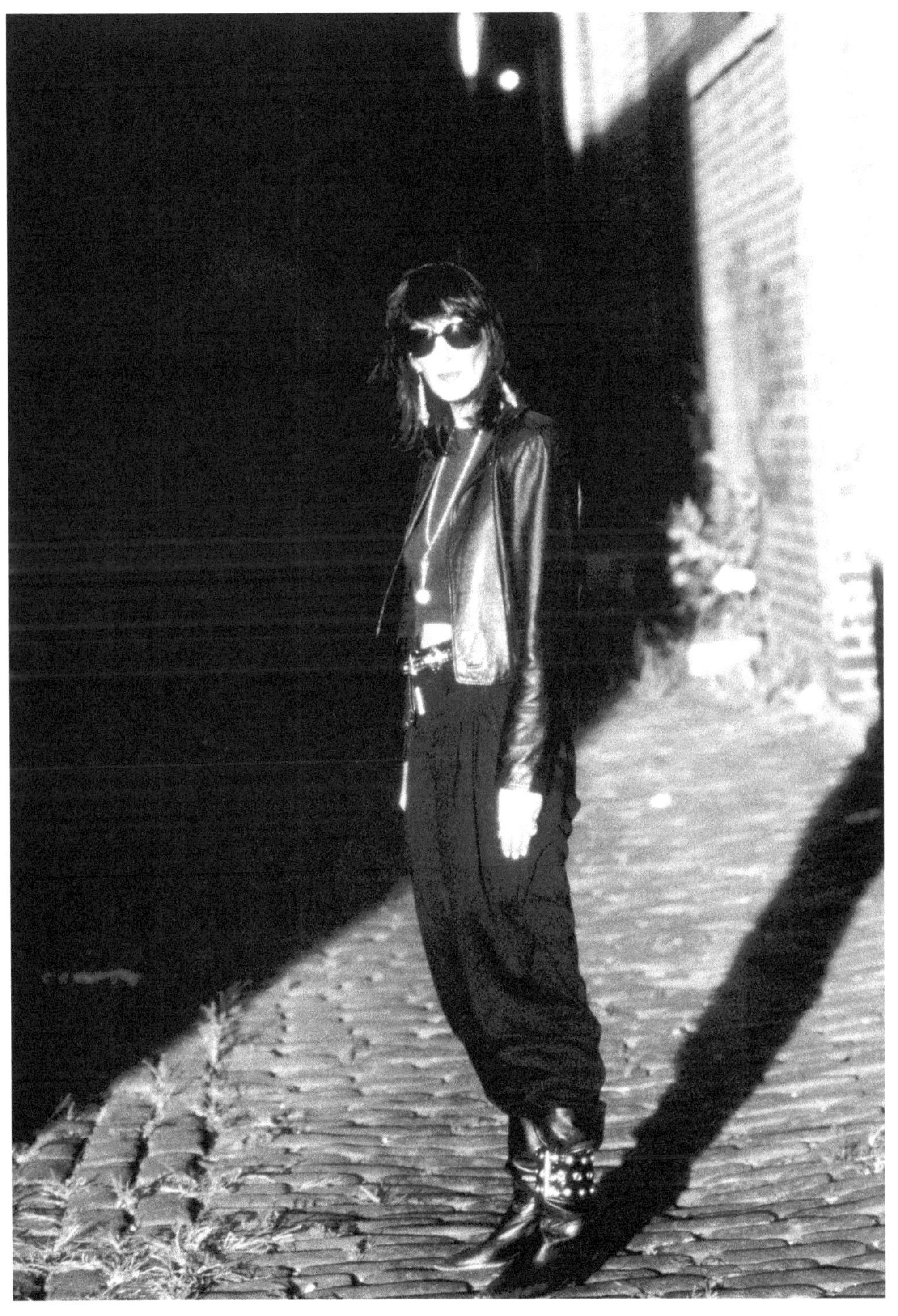

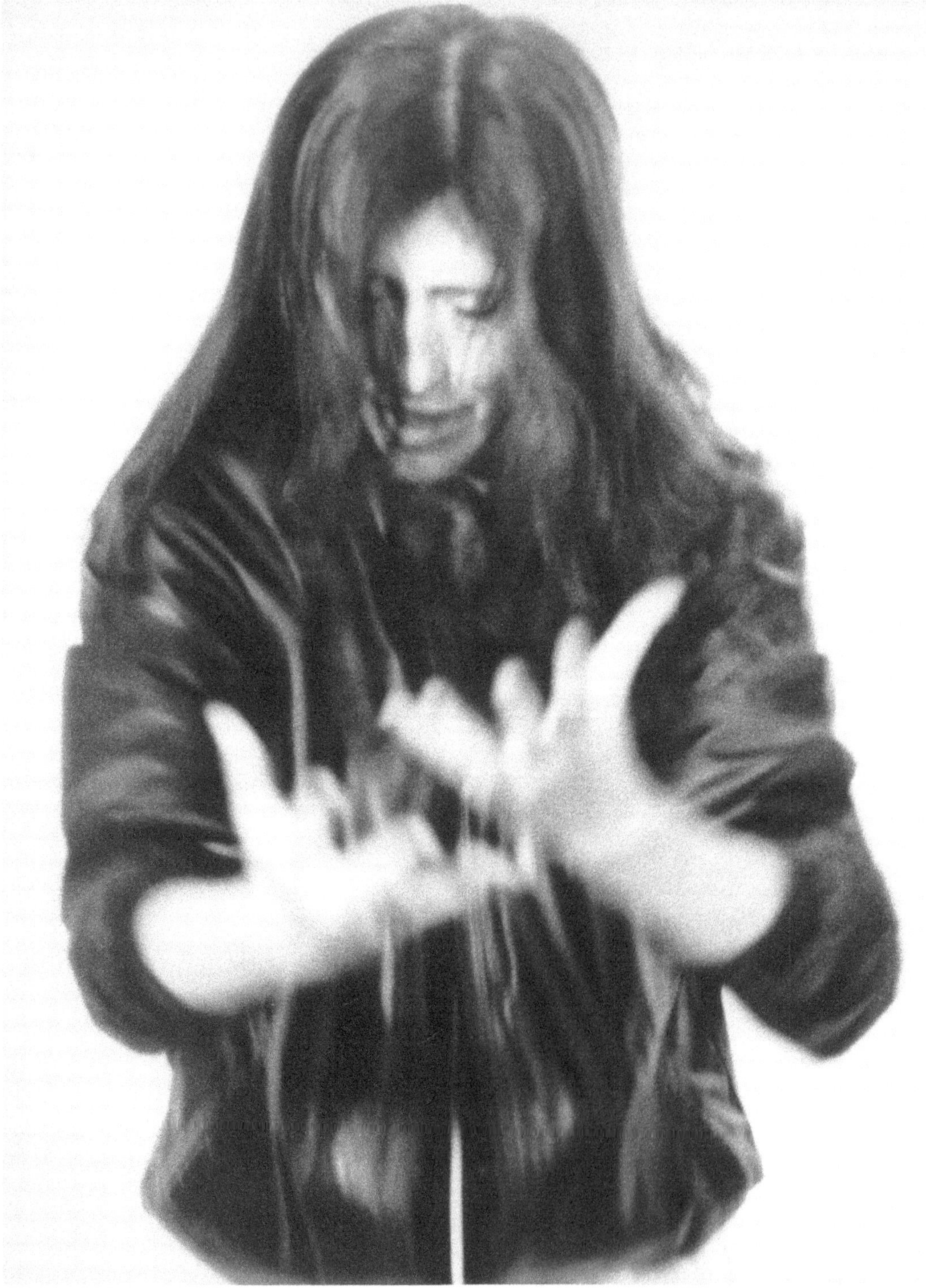

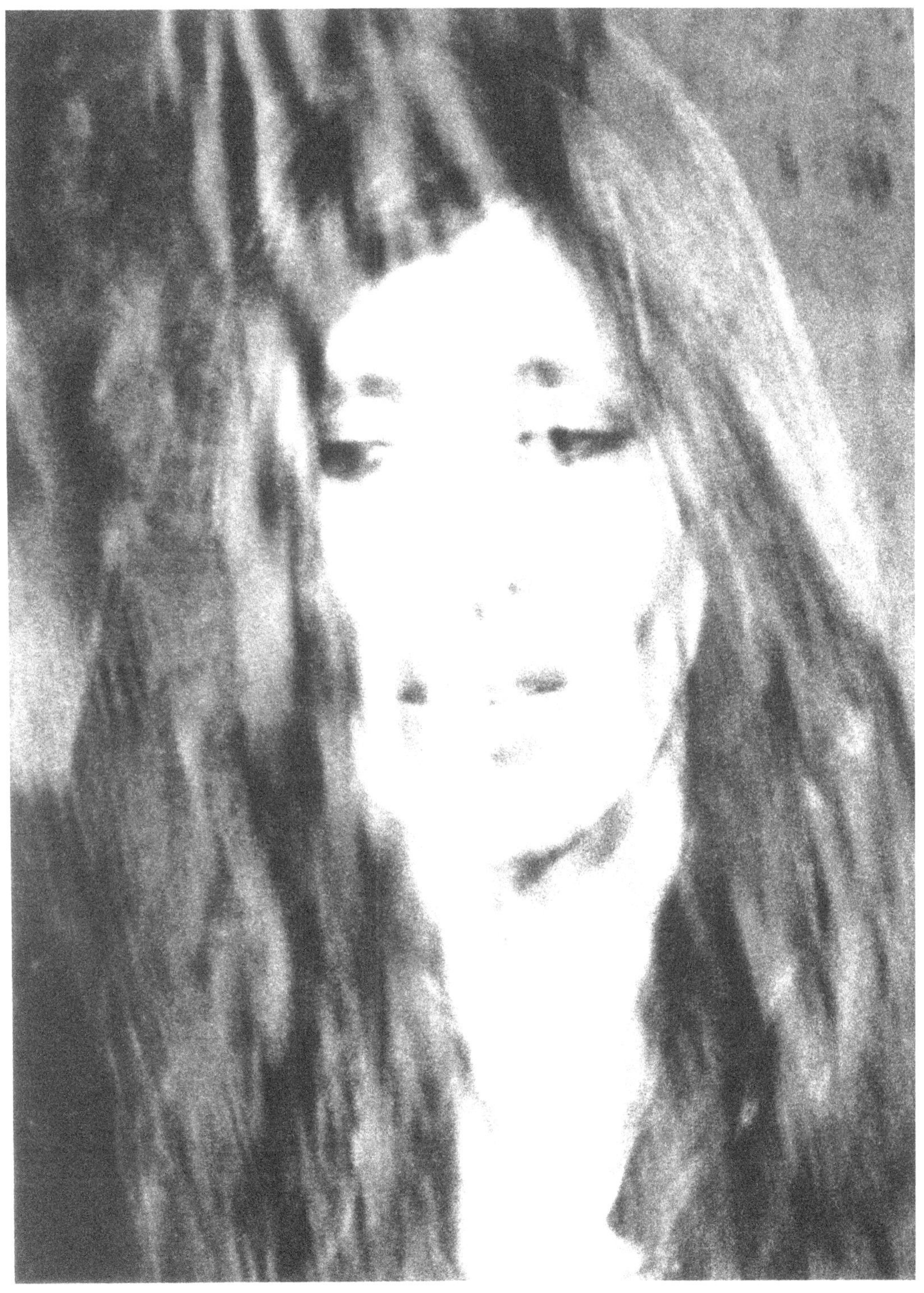

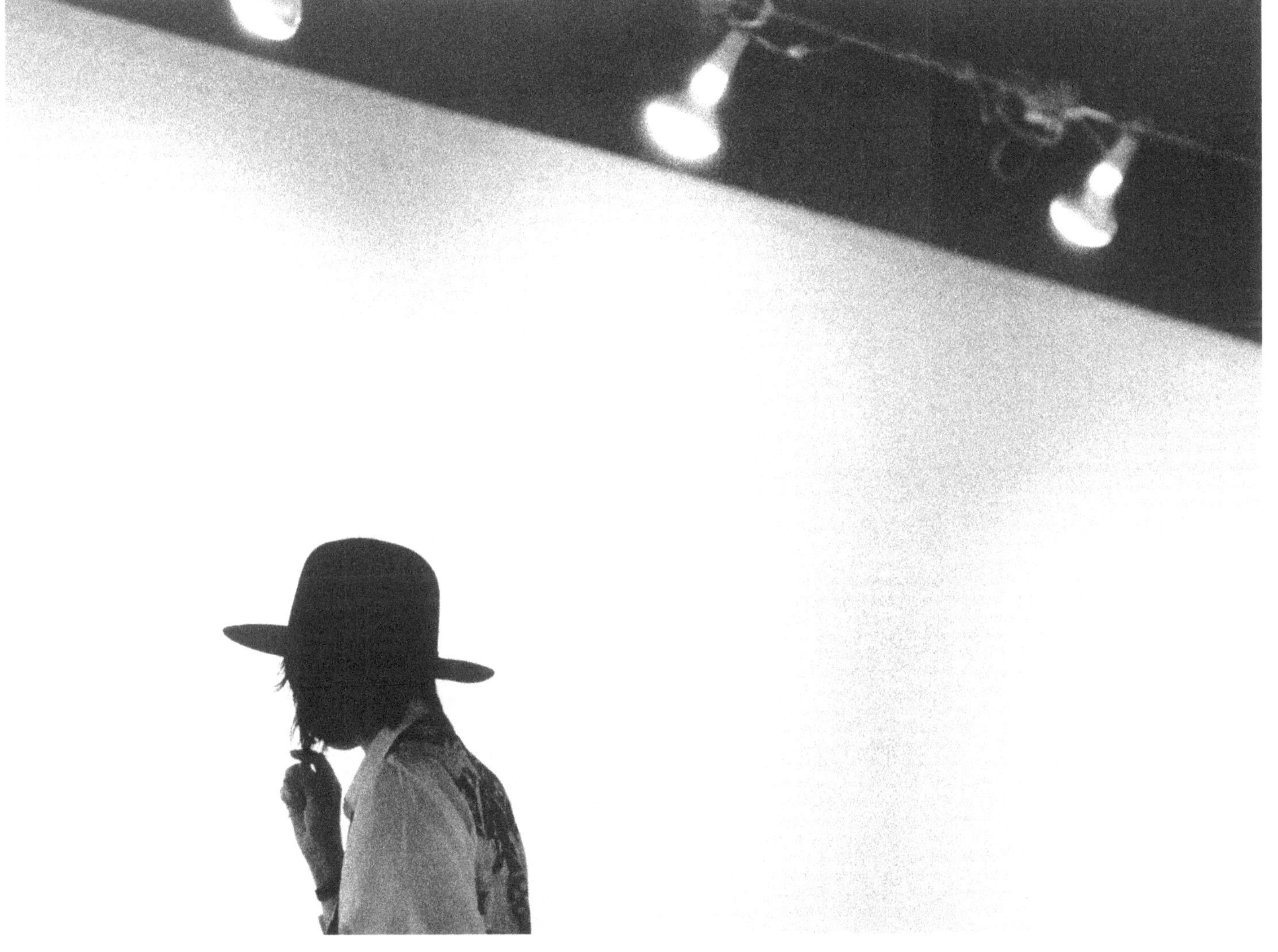

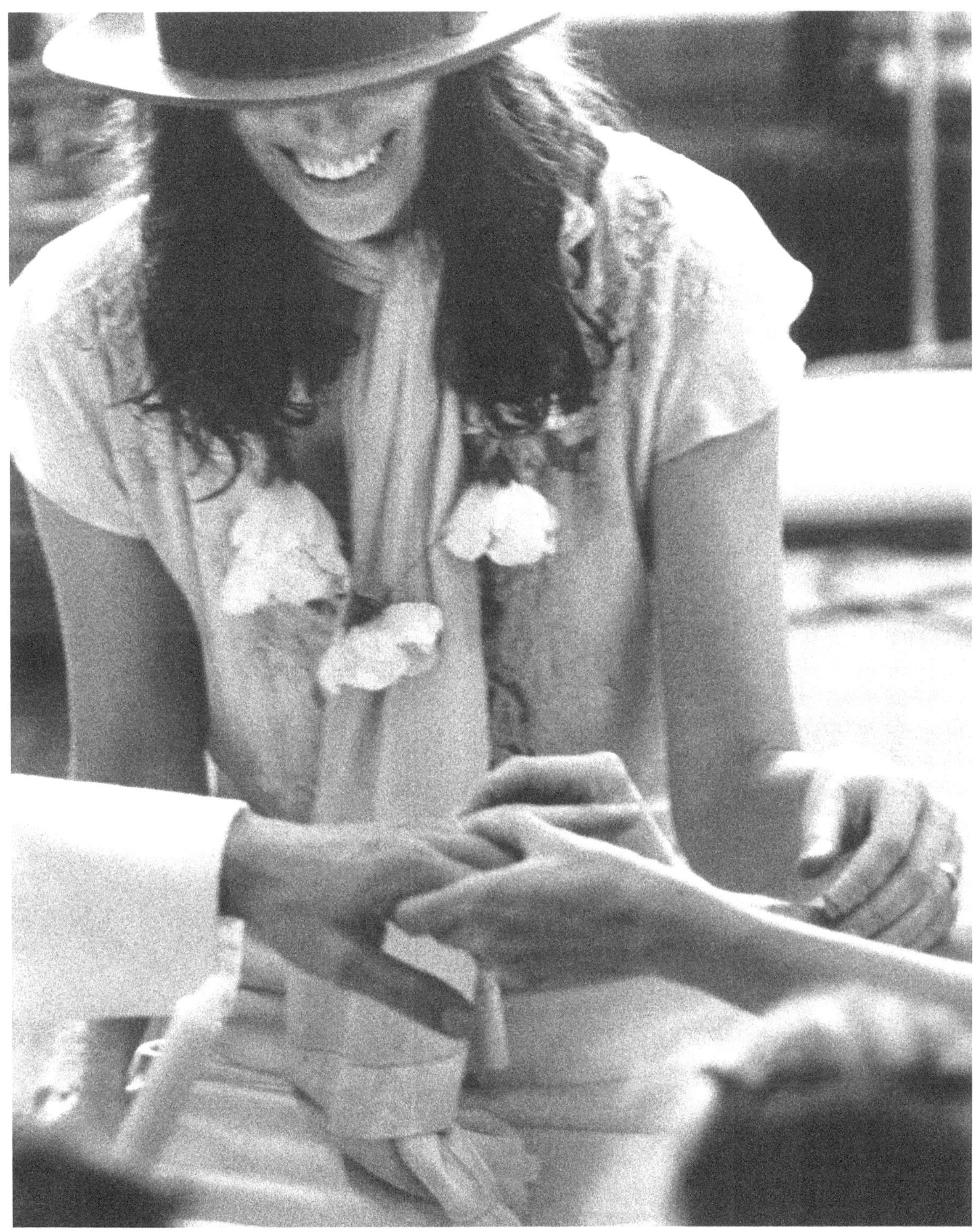

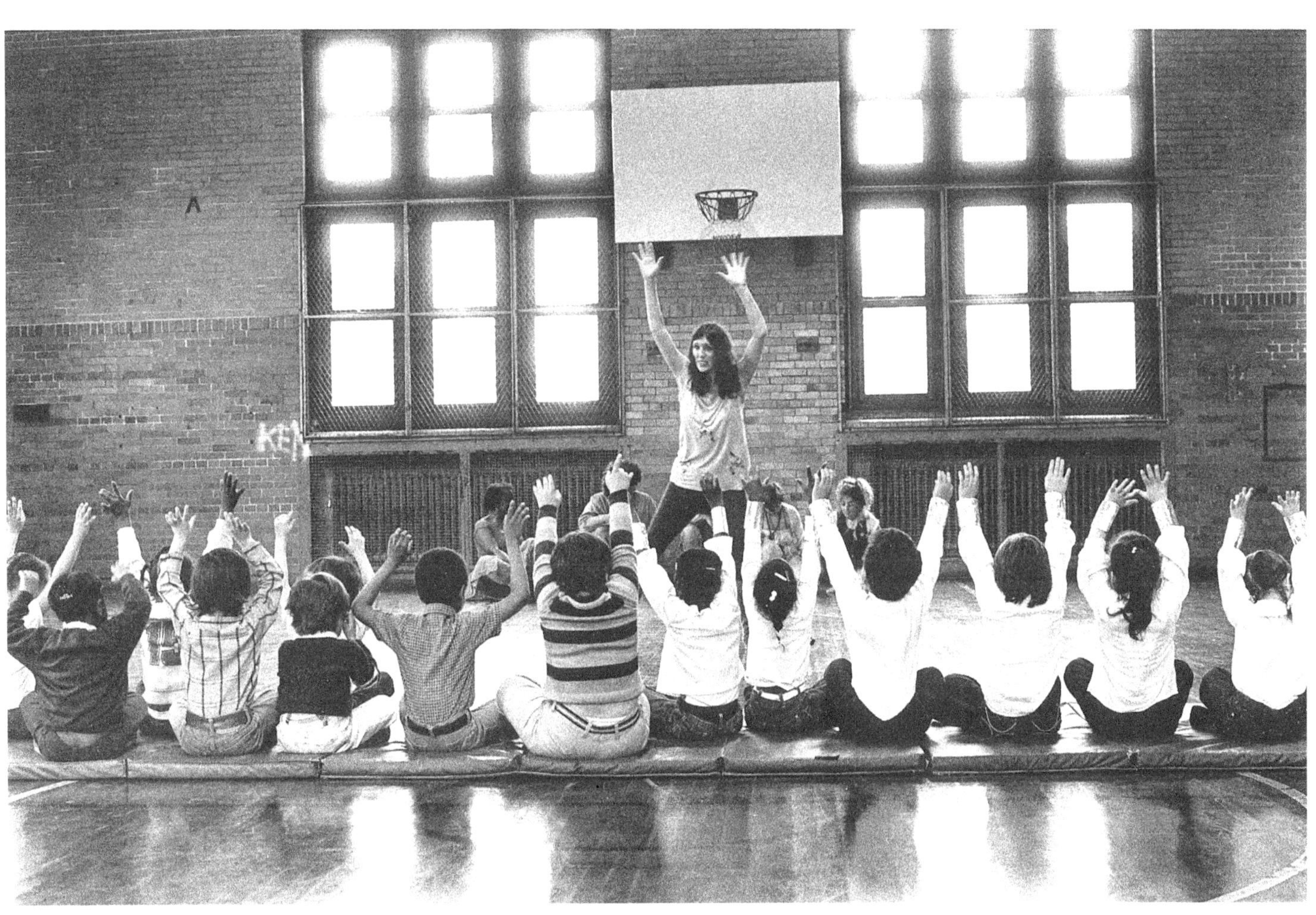

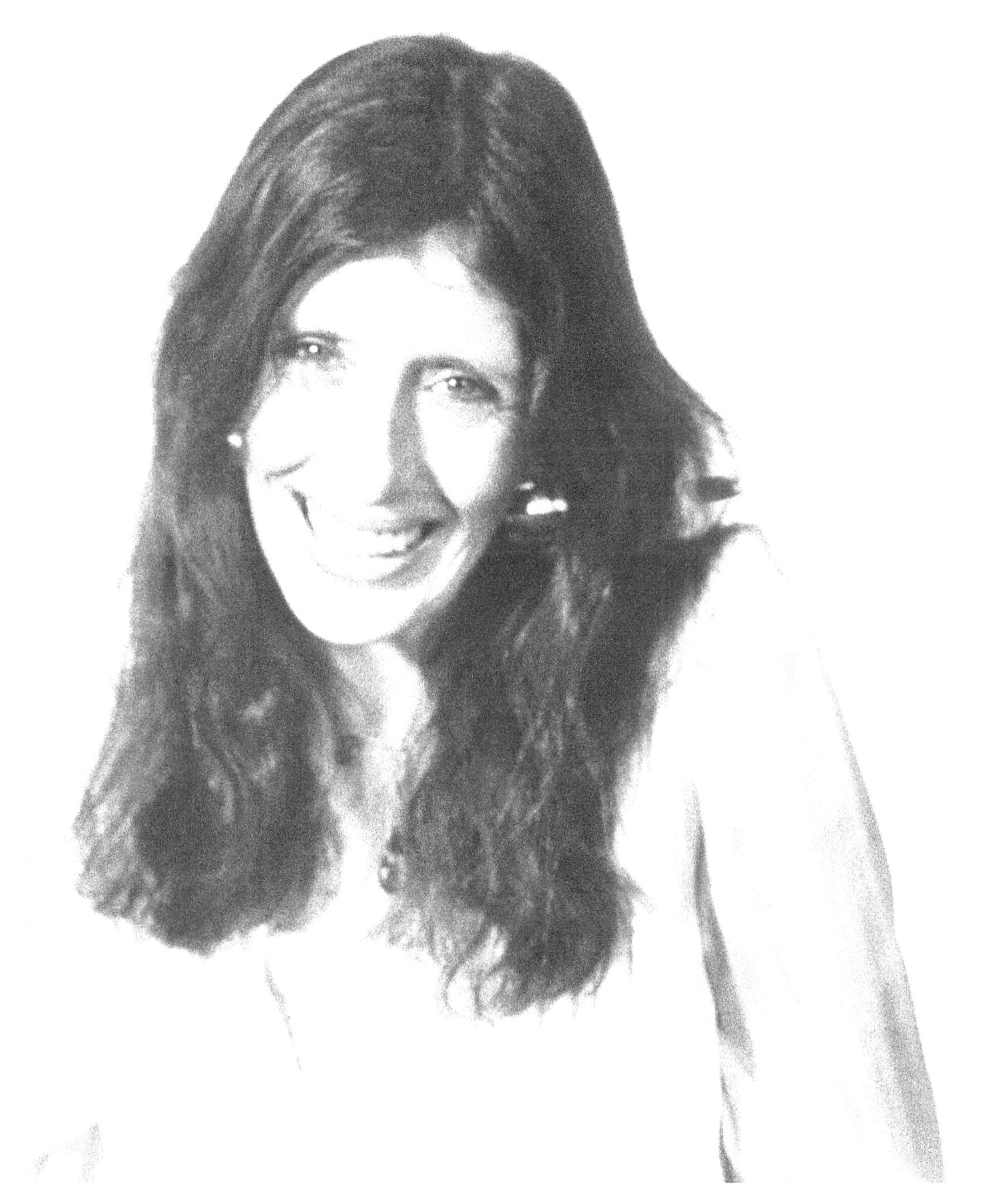

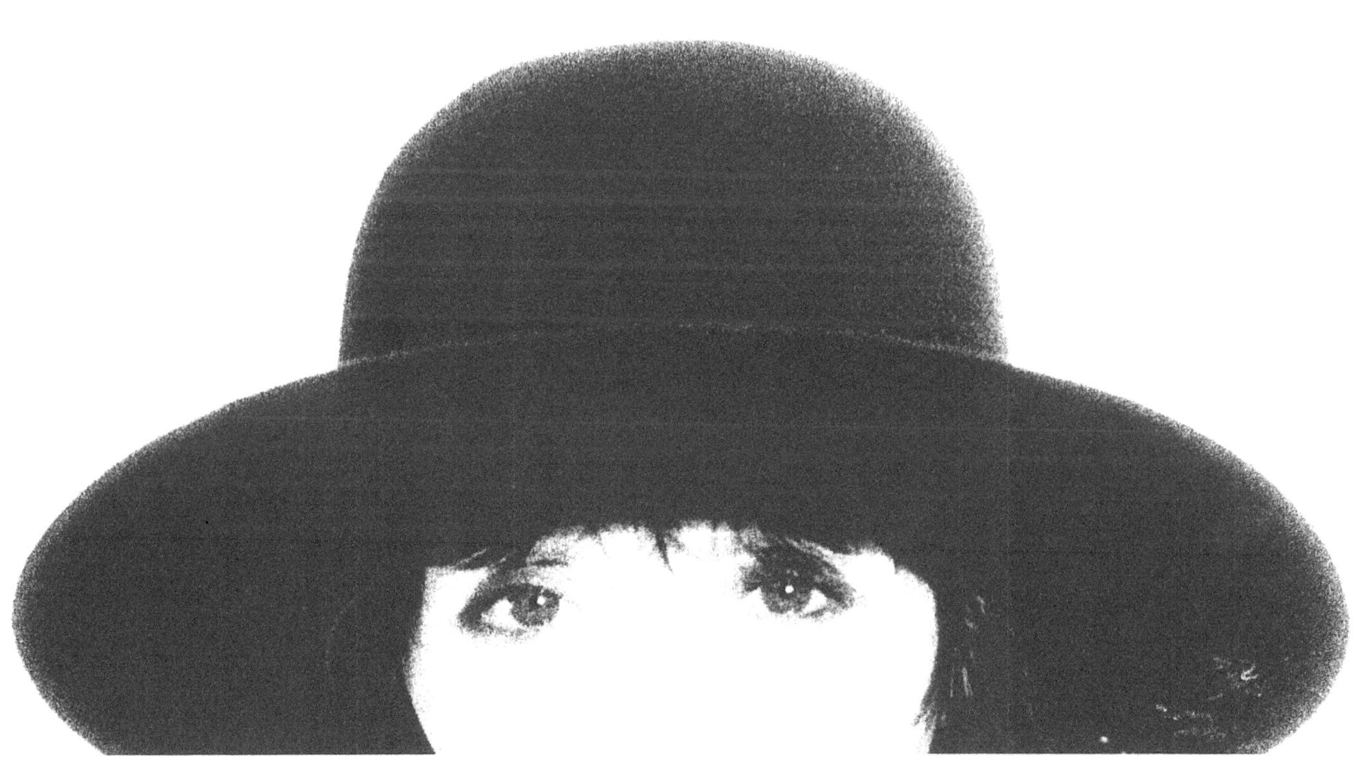

Born and raised on the Jersey shore, Robert Ansell received degrees from the University of Virginia and Yale Law School. He practiced law in New Jersey for 14 years, specializing in the defense of criminal cases. In 1981, he reincarnated without changing bodies (an extremely cost-effective procedure) and began a career in music as a percussionist and producer. He and his wife, Gabrielle Roth, were pioneers in the field of ambient music and produced 16 albums through their label, Raven Recording, Inc. He lived in Manhattan.

www.ingramcontent.com/pod-product-compliance
Lightning Source LLC
Chambersburg PA
CBHW041028050726
47599CB00018B/1900